To Kristina

THE GOD ZONE

"Sail" the world and carry the Kingdom wherever you go!

Blessings

by

Dr. Sherri L. Lewis

The God Zone

Dr. Sherri L. Lewis

~~~

Copyright © 2017 Sherri L. Lewis

All rights reserved. No part of this book may be reproduced in any form or by any means without prior consent of the author, excepting brief quotes used in reviews.

Destiny Publications

5836 Mill Crest Way

Lithonia, GA 30038

This book is licensed for your personal enjoyment only. This book may not be re-sold or given away to other people. If you would like to share this book with another person, please purchase an additional copy for each recipient. Thank you for respecting the hard work of this author.

Dedication

To my big sis, Joyce (Toy Toy). Thanks for your unwavering support, undying love, and never-ending gifts for me and my kids.

Acknowledgements

My first non-fiction book! Wow! I thought this would be the hardest thing to do, but it's actually the easiest thing I've ever written. Thanks to everybody who's been a part of my story and for all who encouraged me to write this book.

Thanks Papa, Jesus, and Holy Spirit for taking me on such an amazing life adventure. Can't wait to see what the future holds. I love Your surprises!

As always, thanks to the best parents on the planet for shaping me into the woman I am today. Thanks always to my big sister, Joyce, for EVERYTHING!

Thanks to my heart friends for being a safe place for me to *be*. Yvette Broughton, Felecia Foster, Felicia Murrell, Rhonda McKnight, Erica Warren, Kathy Soto – thanks for listening to my rants, whining and freak out moments and for always talking me off the wall and loving me to life.

Thanks to my pastors, Steve and Lindy Hale and my missionary directors, Ron and Carolyn Book. I don't have words to express my thanks for your love and support. You guys make me believe I can do anything! How could I not succeed with the four of you in my corner?

Thanks to my Bethel Atlanta family for all your love and support! I love coming home and receiving your hugs, prayers, prophetic words and everything you guys pour out on me. You make me feel like a rock star! Thanks to Tracy and Steve Cooper for being my launching pad in 1st and 2nd year of BASSM.

Thanks to my amazing Bethel Atlanta Cameroon staff for being who you are and doing all you do! Let's take Africa together!!! Love and blessings on all my students and alumni!

Thanks to my new Nigerian family. Much love to Alero Ayida-Otobo. Let's raise reformers together! Love to Femi and Mina Bajomo and Emo and Udy Ntia. Excited to see what God will do through us together.

Much love to my Rosie!

Thanks to everyone reading this. I hope it inspires you to take a huge leap of faith and dance into your destiny!

Table of Contents

One

When I tell the story of my journey from Ivy League-trained doctor to nation-hopping missionary in Africa, I get a variety of responses. From some, I get respect, admiration, and often a request for prayer to be launched into their own God adventure. From others, I get a tight smile with a "bless your heart" or a "that's nice, dear." And some people look at me like I need my head examined.

I have to admit that sometimes when I tell the story, it does sound pretty crazy. Sometimes I feel like God drugged me, or tricked me when I made the decision to move to Cameroon. Who quits their doctor job, puts their stuff on a ship, and gives up everything they know to go live in a little town in West Africa among a bunch of people she met on the Internet?

Crazy me, that's who. Or maybe I should say me – the radical, laid-down lover of Jesus (in the words of my shero Heidi Baker) who would do ANYTHING He asks because I'm head over heels in love with the One who deeply and extravagantly loves me.

What led me to the decision actually makes a bit of sense. I needed *more*. More out of life. Meaning, purpose, destiny…I needed my life to *really* matter. It was somewhat fulfilling to care for my patients as a physician, minister to people in the small Bible study in my den, and write Christian novels. But it wasn't enough. It didn't feel like *it*. Something deep inside me knew it wasn't the reason I was born.

One of the greatest desires of the human heart is to have a sense of purpose – for life to have meaning. Without it, one drifts aimlessly and heartlessly through life, going through the motions, living perfunctorily, but not passionately. I know all too well, because that was my life for many years.

To live passionately and to the fullest, we need a sense of purpose. We need a reason to be – a reason to exist that actually matters. We need to feel like we're having some kind of impact on the world. God created us with this need so that we would seek Him for the very reason we were born.

This can be different things to different people – maybe rescuing young women from sex slavery, saving elephants from extinction or opening an orphanage for destitute children. Such heroic pursuits are normally what come to mind when we think of purpose. But equally important endeavors include being a great wife and mother, teaching kindergarten, or taking care of the elderly in a nursing home. There are as many purposes as there are people on the planet and no dream is more valid than any other.

One of my favorite messages to teach – a life message for me – is the message of purpose and destiny. Without fail, every time I teach it, I'm faced with an onslaught of questions that include, "How am I supposed to discover my purpose and destiny? How do I design a life for myself that's full of meaning? How do I discover God's perfect will for my life? How did you get the courage to go for it?"

These questions are rarely asked casually. When people ask me how they, too, can live a God adventure full of meaning and passion, there's always a sense of desperation in their tone and a pleading in their eyes. People are desperate for purpose.

I answer the questions as best I can, but most of the time, I think people leave with an even greater sense of angst. I can see the wheels turning in their heads. I can feel them thinking, "Well, your story turned out great and inspiring, but can that happen for me? Can I really figure out who I am and why I'm on planet earth? Can I really live my best life? Will God really talk to me and help me live an amazing adventure?"

My answer to all of the above is a resounding, "YES!!!"

God's greatest desire is for each of us to live our best life – in the center of His perfect will and at the height of our purpose. Over the last seven years, I've discovered so much about life, about myself, and about God. I've learned what it is to live an amazing

DR. SHERRI L. LEWIS

adventure, listening to and following His whispers.
I've discovered that He's a loving Father who wants to
see His children's lives filled with meaning.

We were made to change the world. We were
designed to enjoy the reward of pouring out His
goodness that lives within us into the lives of others.
We were created to bring His Kingdom to earth and to
enjoy how amazing that feels. Imagine partnering with
the King of Kings to transform this world into a place
filled with His glory. There's no greater high. There's
no greater joy.

Don't get all religious on me. Not everyone is
called to be a preacher or pastor or evangelist or
"minister." (Actually, we're all called to be ministers,
but not in the way you might think.) There are so
many ways to bring glory to Him and only a few
involve being engaged in what we typically consider
to be full-time "ministry."

I think that's why a lot of Christians shy away
from giving their lives completely to God. The thought
of doing so is often associated with mental images of
pain, suffering and sacrifice. We feel like we're going
to have to give up what we love to live a life of
poverty and limitations, without pleasure or
enjoyment.

I've learned that the exact opposite is true.
When you lay down your life for the life that God has
designed for you, it's better than any life you could

have imagined or created for yourself. Beyond your wildest dreams.

I think this expectation of suffering, poverty and sacrifice comes from our misconception of who God is. Another life message for me is the understanding of the Father heart of God. Growing up in church, most of us get this vision of God as being harsh and difficult, distant and silent, with a long list of do's and don'ts and a standard of living that's impossible for the average human to attain.

If we knew Him as He really is – a good, good Father who's perfect in all His ways – then we'd see things differently. If we knew Him as a Father who loves us with a love that can't be explained in words, then we wouldn't run away from His plans for our lives. We would instead run towards them.

Our loving Father wants to give us a destiny that brings us great joy and fulfillment. The life He has for you is full of joy, abundance, and adventure. Sometimes I wake up in the morning and wander out onto my second floor balcony, overlooking avocado, mango, guava and plantain trees, with the most picturesque view of fluffy clouds gathering around the base of Mt. Cameroon and I can't believe my life!

My life is full of joy, amazing relationships and family, and abundant provision. Every day, I experience deep fulfillment that I didn't think was possible. My "kids" constantly tell me how deeply I'm impacting their lives. I get to see them transform and grow into the most amazing, fiery revivalists.

And yet, if you had told me eight years ago that I would be the Director of a School of Supernatural Ministry in Cameroon with dreams of reaching many other nations in Africa, I never would have believed you. The most I could have hoped for was yearly mission trips to Africa, a large home Bible study, and a stable doctor job that didn't drive me too crazy.

Instead, I'm doing everything I ever dreamed of doing as a child, with the promise of so much more! Why? Because I've given my life to a loving Father who knows the intimate details of *ME*. He knows my dreams, desires, fears, gifts, talents and where my greatest potential lies. And He's put me in a place where I get to be the best version of me.

The One who knows me the best and loves me the most has designed a life for me that's destined to bring me joy and fulfillment. I promise He's got the same thing waiting for you, if you just trust Him with your life.

I hope to prove that to you by the end of this book. I pray that by the time you finish, you'll be ready to lay down your life, take a leap of radical faith, and jump into a God adventure beyond your wildest imaginations.

Hopefully, the story of my journey will lead you into a destiny journey of your own. Let me take you back to where my dreams of purpose and destiny started.

Two

I wrote my first book when I was about five years old – with crayons on brightly colored construction paper. I was lying on the floor in the living room and my mother was in the kitchen. Every few minutes, I ran into the kitchen to ask her how to spell a word. My first grade teacher must have just taught us about the difference between girls and boys or where babies come from or something, because the words I was asking how to spell were all related to male and female anatomy. I asked word after word until finally my mom wiped her hands, came into the living room, and asked, "Sherri, what in the world are you writing?" My mom loves to embarrass me by telling that story.

I have no idea what the story was about, but I've loved writing for as long as I can remember. I wrote fun little stories all through elementary school, dark poems expressing my angst in junior high, dark short stories during my macabre phase in high school, and have always made emotional entries in my journal expressing my thoughts and feelings. I'm such an external processor that I often don't know what I'm thinking or feeling until I write it.

When I was four, my Aunt Jeanette named me, "Miss Black America." In my imaginary world, I was always on a stage, singing, dancing, and making inspiring speeches. In my teens, when it was my turn to clean the den, the room was transformed into a large stage. The vacuum cleaner became my microphone and stand. I played my favorite albums (yes, I'm that old) over and over, singing at the top of my lungs until my mom or some other family member yelled for me to stop.

I used to "play school" with my younger cousins when I babysat them. They had homework assignments, exams, and everything. Me and my siblings "played church" every chance we got. I either preached, sang a solo, or directed the choir. Our backyard, standing-on-the-picnic-table services were always lively and we loved every minute of it until it was time to pass the offering plate. The neighborhood cats and dogs we gathered as our congregation were pretty stingy when it came to tithes and offerings.

Are these just cute, nostalgic stories? Not at all. Everything I used to do – freely expressing myself as a child – were keys and clues to my purpose and destiny. When we're young, we're fresh from heaven, uninfluenced by societal pressures, not limited by externally imposed fears, and unhindered by internally generated doubts and lies. In our childhood, we're the purest version of our true selves.

As I've begun living my purpose and destiny, I realize I'm doing all the things I used to love to do as a child – preaching, teaching, singing, and writing books. Those were my first clues about the life I was born to live. If you think back to your own childhood pretend games and hobbies, I'd bet they're clues to your discovering your own purpose and destiny.

As I got a little older, all I dreamed about was becoming an artist. I wanted to do all things creative – dance, choreograph, sing, write songs, write books, play piano and compose – anything that allowed me to express all the melodies, harmonies, lyrics, stories, and movement that lived and moved inside of me.

When it came time to go to college, I only looked at one – Howard University. When I visited, I only visited one place, the School of Fine Arts. I went into one of the practice rooms and played the piano for almost an hour (I'd played since the age of five). I heard people singing in the practice rooms next door and decided to try out the acoustics with my voice. A keyboard player heard me singing *a capella* and asked if I wanted some accompaniment. He was cute and was a bonified college dude, so I agreed. He played and I sang and it felt like a scene right out of my favorite teenage movie and television show, *Fame* (I'm really dating myself here).

I was hooked. My decision was easy. I was going to Howard University as a Fine Arts major. I only needed to decide whether to pursue piano, vocals, or creative writing. Could I do all three?

When I got back home, I sat down and had a serious conversation with my father about my future. Before I go any further, I MUST say that I'm a Daddy's girl, through and through. I adore my father. I attribute my intimate relationship with Father God to my relationship with my dad, who always demonstrated love and devotion to me and my siblings. He was always there, always provided, and is the most reliable, steadfast person you ever want to meet. Me and my sisters and brother grew up believing there was nothing in life we couldn't conquer.

That being said, in his protective love, my father expressed his concerns about me being a Fine Arts major. He didn't want me to end up being a "starving artist." He said I could always do my little "artsy stuff" on the side, but I should pick a major that would give me a stable career. I was heartbroken, but I trusted my dad and I've always been a very obedient child.

For the first time ever, I had to consider a life other than that of a creative artist. I tried to figure out what else could bring me the same kind of happiness as singing, playing piano, and writing. I thought about how much I love talking to and helping people, so I decided to become a psychologist.

I presented the idea to my dad and he said I should become a "real doctor." Apologies to all the amazing psychologists out there! Did I mention he was one of the best rheumatologists in the city and taught internal medicine at the medical university? He said I should go to medical school to become a psychiatrist.

And so this creative, free-spirited artist – instead of ending up as a voice or piano major in the School of Fine Arts – became a premed/Zoology major in "The Valley," the row of science buildings at the lowest part of Howard University.

Fortunately (or unfortunately), I'm pretty smart and can excel at anything I put my mind to. Four years later, I graduated second in my department, summa cum laude with a 3.8 GPA. I had done research the last two years of undergrad and got a full scholarship to the University of Pennsylvania as an MD/PhD student. My parents raised me to be the very best at whatever I decide to do.

In my first year of medical school, I was MISERABLE...

Because that's what happens when you violate your truest self, dreams, and desires to become something you were never meant to be.

During that time, I got involved with an intercessory, worship, prophetic ministry called Intercessors for Christ. I had grown up as a devoted Baptist girl and had never been exposed to the gifts of the Holy Spirit. It was quite a revelation to learn about the prophetic. Who knew that God actually talked to people?! A lot! In my early twenties, I was trained as an intercessor and worship leader, and learned how to hear the voice of God and prophesy with passion and accuracy.

During that time, I got many prophetic words about my life and future. The crazy thing was, only one – out of hundreds – was anything science related. God spoke about me being a worshipper that would bring down the heavens. I got words about going to the nations, carrying the gospel of the Kingdom. I received prophecies about writing books that would transform people's hearts. Others were about me preaching in stadiums internationally and pouring out the power of God in miracles and healing. I got MANY words about ministering to and changing the lives of young people in Africa.

I was excited for the life God kept inviting me into through any and every prophetic voice around me. The words resounded within the depths of my soul and spirit. God was talking about everything I had ever wanted to be and do. He was talking to that little girl in me who still loved singing, writing, preaching, and teaching. He KNEW me. Of course He did. Every prophetic word spoke to the dreams I'd always had, but had buried to follow my father's dreams for my life. The more prophetic words I got, the more my dreams woke up inside of me.

The most beautiful thing was, everything God spoke about me was already in me. He had already equipped and gifted me with everything I needed to become the person He was talking about. That's true for all of us. When God formed you, He put everything you'd need on the inside of you to fulfill your destiny. Your gifts, talents, natural inclinations and desires are huge clues to your destiny. Doesn't that make sense? That He would fashion us with the gifts and with the deep desires to be exactly what He ordained us to be before the foundations of the earth?

I *wanted* to be the person God said I was supposed to be. But I was in medical school. The life I was living looked nothing like the life God was talking about.

I actually started writing my first novel during my first year of medical school. It was about a young woman who wanted to become a professional dancer, but her parents persuaded her to get a master's degree so she could become a psychologist. Sound familiar? Writing had always been my catharsis and I was working out my issues of feeling forced into a career I didn't love. With the rigors of medical school, I didn't have the time to devote to writing the book. I put it away and planned to finish it "later."

As my years in medical school progressed, so did my misery. Fortunately, I have a photographic memory. I have to admit I did medical school as a correspondence course. I picked up my syllabus at the beginning of a course and then showed up to take exams. I studied hard and learned all the information, but didn't go to class most of the time. Instead, I prayed, read the Word and fell deeply in love with God.

Intercessors for Christ met five nights a week, about forty miles away from Philadelphia in Wilmington, Delaware. We prayed and worshipped an average of three hours a night, but sometimes we got so captivated by God that we stayed until the wee hours of the morning. I couldn't get enough of it. I loved leading worship, loved praying, and absolutely loved the prophetic. This was a special time in my life – falling in love with ministry and with a God I had never known in my life as a Christian. I was completely intoxicated by His presence. My time in Intercessors for Christ laid the foundation for everything I am in ministry today.

Many people would stop at this point in my story and think, "Well, that's not for me. Three hours every night, five nights a week? That's too intense! It doesn't take all that."

If you're thinking, "There's no way I could ever do that," it's probably true. That was **my** preparation for **my** journey. It prepared me for who I'm called to be as a minister of the gospel of the Kingdom. Not everyone has that call on their life. If that's not your call, that level of intensity may not be something God requires of you. Before you decide to put this book down, thinking, "If I've got to pray for many hours, five nights a week, I'd better stick with my 'regular, Christian Life'," give me a chance to explain.

There's a teaching I've grown to love referred to as the 7 Mountains or 7 Spheres of Influence, given to us by Johnny Enlow[1] and Lance Wallnau[2]. They propose that there are seven major spheres of influence, which include religion, business and technology, arts and entertainment, media, government, family, and education. I won't go into much detail except to say that each of us is called to one or more of these mountains – to invade and conquer with the reality of the Kingdom and bring about cultural transformation.

I'm called to the religious mountain (and of course arts and entertainment) so my training in prayer, worship, and the prophetic was/is intense. You may be called to a different mountain and your training may be just as intense, but in a different way. Maybe your preparation will involve hours of study to obtain a PhD so you can revolutionize the educational system of your city or nation. It might involve hours and hours of research and development to produce a ground-breaking product that transforms the world of technology. Maybe, like Stephen Curry, it's spending hour after hour shooting 3-pointers, training to be an NBA star so you can represent Christ on an international level.

Whatever the training, I guarantee that no matter how challenging or time consuming, it won't be difficult. Remember you have a loving Father that's preparing you for the exact life you were born to live. Just like my spending hours in the presence of God was intoxicating for me, your training and preparation will bring you the greatest joy. It'll be something you love doing so much that you'll be able to do it for hours on end, every day, without getting tired.

I continued to get more and more prophetic words, outlining a life that was better than my wildest dreams. I was stuck in medical school, but in my heart, I was building up the faith to live an amazing life of worship, prayer, preaching and going to the nations.

Finally, in my third year at U Penn, I'd had enough. I was ready to take a leap of faith and become everything God said I was supposed to be. I decided to drop out of school, somehow without regard for how I would support myself or how I would pay back the tens of thousands of dollars of tuition and fees. If I didn't finish school and begin a career that included teaching and research, I had to pay back the scholarship money.

I had no idea how I was supposed to live this life of destiny that God was talking about all the time. I just knew I wanted it. And I didn't want to be a doctor. What was I supposed to do to become this great woman of faith, ministering to young people in Africa?

When I told my counselor at U Penn that I was quitting medical school to become a full-time minister, she gave me a worried look and kept asking me questions that made me know she thought I was having a nervous breakdown. After about thirty minutes of me cheerily answering her questions, trying to convince her I wasn't crazy, she finally told me that I didn't have to drop out completely. I could take a year off, figure some things out and come back and finish medical school if I wanted to.

I decided to take a year off and hear from God.

[1]*The Seven Mountain Prophecy: Unveiling the Coming Elijah Revolution*, Johnny Enlow, 2008

[2]*Turn the World Upside Down: Discipling the Nations with the Seven Mountain Strategy*, Lance Wallnau and Michael Maiden 2011

DR. SHERRI L. LEWIS

Three

The first issue to settle was how I was going to eat and pay my rent. My scholarship gave me a generous monthly stipend that took care of all my needs. With it suddenly gone, I had to find a way to live. There was no way I could ask my parents for support. My dad thought I had lost my mind and minced no words letting me know he thought I was making a terrible decision.

My poor parents. I had excitedly told them everything that was happening to me in Intercessors for Christ. They were convinced I had gotten sucked into a cult and had lost all my good sense. To the average person, I'm sure that's exactly how things looked.

There are many world-changing, radical revivalists whose stories I've read who have had a similar experience. When they started chasing after God, everyone who knew and loved them thought they had completely lost it and that such fanaticism was a sign of insanity rather than devotion to God. It's only after the person becomes a spiritual legend that everyone looks back and understands what was happening in the person's life.

After my last stipend check came, I didn't miss a meal and never felt a moment of lack. God gave me a job as a Drug Prevention Specialist for the Philadelphia Public School District (My boss was the older sister of the leader of Intercessors for Christ). I went into elementary, junior high and high schools and taught about abstinence, self-esteem and self-worth, life goals and decision-making, etc. and developed a curriculum to empower high school students to be their very best.

I was the "Condom Lady" at West Philadelphia High School and used the opportunity to love on young people and pour into their lives at such a critical stage in their development. They'd drop by to pick up free condoms and had to endure my lectures on abstinence and avoiding sexually transmitted diseases. I had these horrible pictures I showed them to scare them away from ever having sex. They'd end up staying for hours talking about their family issues, fears, dreams, struggles and relationships.

I enjoyed the kids, the pay was good, and I had a great boss and co-workers, but I still had to settle the matter of what I was going to do about medical school and the loans.

The artist in me wanted to "live" so I rented a huge loft apartment in an art district in Philadelphia. I went into debt renovating and decorating the place. I had no idea how I was supposed to make all those amazing prophetic words come true and absolutely nothing was happening. I was going to work every day, but wasn't any closer to a life of arts and ministry.

I didn't know what to do with myself. God had given the prophetic words, but He hadn't said how or when the things would happen. To be honest, He never told me to drop out of medical school. I was excited and wanted to obey the prophetic words, but I wasn't following any specific instructions when I took that year off.

My dad offered to help me get out of debt if I would go back to school. We laugh about it now. He was so glad to have that bargaining chip. I went back and finished the fourth year of medical school, but dropped the PhD program, because I didn't want to do research. Maybe the year off was just about me figuring out that I didn't want to complete the PhD program.

During that year off, I married one of the guys in the prayer ministry and we were trying to figure out life together. We preached, prayed, prophesied, and had God dreams together. Unfortunately, growing up as a sheltered church girl, I didn't know much about choosing a mate. Somehow, in my mind, everyone had grown up in a middle class home with two loving parents who were devoted to giving them the best life possible.

I never realized that just because a person may be a spiritual giant, their natural life could be so broken and fractured, it could prevent them from becoming all that God has called them to be. I didn't understand that marrying a man who had grown up in seventeen different foster homes with a tumultuous childhood wasn't a good choice at all. I had this thing about rescuing people and it affected my choice of a mate.

I don't want to dwell on that part of my story too much, except for the things you can learn from it. I honor and respect my ex-husband, so you'll have to excuse me for being vague about the details of our broken marriage.

After I graduated medical school, I matriculated through a three-year, Family Medicine Residency program at the University of Maryland at Baltimore. I loved delivering babies and enjoyed being a physician and taking care of my patients, but once again, I had to bury my passion for arts and ministry.

I'm persuaded that when we go against the deep desires and dreams of our heart – when we don't follow the path that God has ordained for us – we lose ourselves. I think we die a little bit every day. I know I did.

Those were good times though. My family medicine residency was stimulating and challenging and I was in a great program with a great director, faculty, and colleagues.

After my residency program, God gave me the perfect first job on staff at a Family Medicine residency program at the Medical University of South

Carolina in Charleston (MUSC). I got to teach residents, see patients, and also did some research. God blessed me in that the teaching and research parts of the position allowed me to pay off the scholarship from medical school. I only had to pay back the loans I had to take out for the fourth year, when I was no longer on scholarship.

After three years of working at MUSC, that old, familiar misery that had been chasing me ever since I decided to go Premed/Zoology instead of Fine Arts started creeping in. Living in that misery from age seventeen to twenty-nine at this point, I learned a valuable life lesson that has become one of the foundations of my teaching on purpose and destiny. That is simply this – you will NEVER be truly happy unless you're doing what you were born to do.

Going to work every day was an effort. You know that feeling, don't you? The drudgery of waking up every morning, dreading work. You look around for yourself, but you can't find *you*. You may be good at what you do – as I was – but it still isn't fulfilling. I was a competent, caring doctor to my patients. They felt loved and well cared for. But I felt empty and dead inside.

During my time in South Carolina, I met one of my best friends, Yvette, and we started chasing God together. As often as we could, we drove from South Carolina to North Carolina to visit a prophetic ministry called Morningstar Ministries. They had prophetic presbytery after every service and Yvette and I loved to sit in the little booths to hear what God was saying to us through the three people on the prophetic team.

It was the same as during my days at Intercessors for Christ. All the prophetic words I got were about arts and ministry and going to the nations. NOTHING about medicine. I developed a deep, inner frustration. God was always talking to me about this amazing life I longed to live, but I couldn't see how to get there.

As much as I loved my patients and my practice, I was itching for a new city. My parents had moved to Atlanta and my sister was already living there, so I began looking for a job. God blessed me with a job as the student health doctor at Georgia State University and I was able to move to a city that better fit my personality and taste.

Unfortunately, my marriage was failing miserably. It was a difficult, challenging time, but the pain of it drew me into deeper intimacy with God. I learned to cry and worship at the same time. I learned to trust God that even in the midst of the worst pain imaginable, I could feel His love for me. No matter how bad things were, He was *with* me.

I was also still miserable being a doctor. Changing cities and jobs didn't fix the deep, inner frustration that only seemed to be growing. Nothing would fix it except for me being true to myself and to the call on my life. I needed to become the person God had created me to be and live the life He was talking about in all those prophetic words I had been getting for about ten years.

During that time, one of my spiritual fathers, Apostle Peterson, moved from his home in Canada to Ft. Lauderdale, Florida. I had met him during my days at Intercessors for Christ. He had been the one to introduce me to the message of the Kingdom and imparted so much into my life. He deepened my love for intercession and the prophetic and his teachings gave me a voracious appetite for the Word of God. Everything I learned from him took me into a deeper revelation of who Jesus is as King and what it means to be an ambassador of the Kingdom of heaven, called to establish the Kingdom here on earth.

While in Florida, Apostle Peterson's wife passed away, suddenly and tragically. I traveled to Florida to be with him and their six children immediately after she passed. In spite of his overwhelming grief, being with Apostle Peterson reminded me of all the prophetic words sitting in my prophetic journals, gathering dust in my hall closet. I wanted to get away from my misery at my job and the misery my marriage had become. I realized life was too short to not live and then die.

A few months later, Apostle was ready to push forward with his ministry. I was in a bad state of mind and desperately needed change. My heart ached to live the life God was talking about in all my prophetic words, so I quit my job and moved to Florida to help with his ministry.

Understandably, things were pretty chaotic for him and his children, and things didn't work out ministry wise. I moved back to Georgia and took a job as the doctor at a women's prison in Hawkinsville, GA. It was a town that if you blinked twice while you were driving through it, you'd miss it. I wasn't excited about living in such a rural area and I certainly wasn't excited about working in a prison!

But because of some horrible things that had happened at the end of my marriage, I was dead broke – almost bankrupt – and it was the only job available.

Turns out, I loved prison ministry – I mean medicine. I guess I loved it because it was just that, ministry. God miraculously blessed me to move from that tiny, one-stoplight town in Hawkinsville to be the doctor at the women's prison in Atlanta. It was a highly sought after location and all the physicians in the prison medicine system all over Georgia wanted it. Most of us were stuck in tiny, rural towns and when the Atlanta doctor said she was leaving, everyone was vying for the spot. I was the newest doctor in the system, but I got the job.

As you see the miraculous ways God provided for me over the years, no matter what decisions I made, you'll have to agree with me that I'm His favorite! I say that jokingly, but in my heart of hearts, I truly believe it. I've always had an extraordinary amount of favor on my life and Daddy God has always taken the best care of me.

I worked at Atlanta Metro Women's Prison for almost five years, becoming progressively more miserable as the years passed. I loved ministering to my patients. I spent long sessions with them, talking about their lives and the decisions they'd made that landed them there. I prayed with them, counseled them, and loved on them. At the end of our sessions, I tended to their medical needs. I loved the ministry aspects of the job, but it still didn't feed the deep desire in me for more.

Me and my bestie and fellow God chaser, Yvette, who had also moved to Atlanta, started a Bible study. I wanted to teach the people everything I had learned about intercession, worship, and the prophetic. I wanted to share what I understood about the Kingdom of God. I wanted to lead people into deep intimacy with the Father and get them filled with the Holy Spirit. It was a small Bible study, never more than ten women, but at least it fulfilled some of the desire in my heart for ministry.

I started putting together a curriculum to teach the message of the Kingdom and all the principles I'd learned over the years. Yvette and I dreamed so much about ministry. We were convinced that we were supposed to be part of a great revival prophesied to come to Atlanta and spread throughout the entire Southeast region of the United States.

Not long after we started the Bible study, Yvette introduced me to Bethel Church and Bill Johnson in Redding, California. She recommended his book, *When Heaven Invades Earth*, saying it had changed her whole life.

I was depressed and didn't pay much attention to her rantings about Bill Johnson. One day, she sent me a link to one of his podcasts. She insisted that if I refused to read, at least I could listen. I don't remember which podcast I listened to first. I just remember that everything Bill Johnson said resonated with the deep places in me. He reminded me of Apostle Peterson and everything I had learned and loved about the message of the Kingdom.

I devoured his podcasts and others from Bethel Church, sometimes listening to two or three a day. The more I listened, the more it resonated. I was excited because a lot of what they were preaching was scribbled in the Kingdom curriculum I was writing. I couldn't believe that someone was speaking my language!

Yvette and I had become frustrated with trying to find Kingdom churches that taught the principles I had learned in Intercessors for Christ and from Apostle Peterson. We had become bored with church as usual and it had gotten to the point that we rarely went, unless we were driving to Charlotte to attend Morningstar.

It wasn't that we didn't try to go to church. When we visited churches, we'd enter with the hope of finding the right place for us. By the time the people were jumping and shouting, or the pastor was preaching and screeching about prosperity and money, we'd be sneaking out the back door. God and every pastor, please forgive me for walking out of church so regularly, but I was so hungry for more. I had been exposed to the Kingdom, the prophetic, extravagant worship and intimacy and to this God who was different and exciting and miraculous. That's what we were looking for and we couldn't seem to find it anywhere.

So when we "discovered" Bill Johnson and Bethel, I finally felt fulfilled. My crazy, God-chasing self was trying to figure out how I was going to quit my job and sell everything to move to Redding, California to go to their School of Supernatural Ministry. I HAD to go to that school.

Then one day, when I listened to the podcast, Bill Johnson was releasing a couple, Steve and Lindy Hale, to come and start the Bethel Atlanta School of Supernatural Ministry. I screamed and picked up the phone to call Yvette. We were stunned and excited. No one could convince us that we hadn't singlehandedly prayed Bethel Church to Atlanta.

I didn't have to quit my job and sell my house and move. Bethel School of Supernatural Ministry was coming to me.

Four

We heard the Bethel Redding podcast releasing the Hale's to start Bethel Atlanta, but we had no idea how to find them. There was nothing about it on the Bethel website and there were no further mentions of it on the podcast. We were distraught that Bethel was happening in Atlanta and we couldn't find it.

We checked the Bethel Church website from time to time to see if there was any announcement, but there wasn't. We did find something though. We checked Bill Johnson's itinerary, hoping and praying he was scheduled to come preach somewhere in Atlanta. He didn't have anything scheduled for Atlanta, but we did see that on my birthday, January 13, 2008, he was slated to be in Webb, Alabama. A quick MapQuest check showed us it was only three hours away. That was close enough for us.

Me and Yvette – ever the God chasers – jumped in the car to go hear him speak. Before he preached, he gave away books and I was gifted with a copy of *Face to Face With God* for my birthday. After service, I went to talk to the Bethel School of Supernatural Ministry (BSSM) student team traveling with him to see if I could get any info on Bethel Atlanta.

The students traveling had divided into two teams and some had been sent to minister at another church. When I asked a student if he knew anything about this couple, the Hale's, who had launched Bethel Atlanta, he pointed to a pretty, young woman at the end of the row of prayer ministers. "That's their daughter, Lauren Brownlee."

Seriously? Wow…We spoke to Lauren and got the exact location and meeting time of Bethel Atlanta church and made plans to visit the next week. Lauren was actually supposed to have gone with the other team with her husband, but things didn't work out and she ended up in Webb. All for me, God's favorite, of course.

When I visited Bethel Atlanta for the first time, my ten years of churchlessness ended. I had found my home in a bunch of Kingdom seekers who were having church in the Hale's house, about fifty minutes from my home. I attended the church from that Sunday in January and enrolled in the very first class of Bethel Atlanta School of Supernatural Ministry (BASSM) when it was launched in September.

Can I just say that BASSM was everything? It was the perfect preparation for what I'm doing now. It was the perfect launch into my destiny. It reinforced the concepts of the Kingdom I had studied since my days with Apostle Peterson and Intercessors for Christ.

I learned a new approach to the prophetic that reflected God's heart more than the previous way I had been trained. I learned about the Father heart of God and identity. Those teachings radically changed everything about my relationship with Him.

The worship was some of the most amazing I had ever experienced. It was pure, sweet, radical, extravagant and at times crazy and wild. And the environment of community and love was something I had never experienced before in any church.

I enjoyed EVERY moment of it, but I was still becoming more and more miserable with my life as a doctor.

I'm a prophecy magnet. I don't know what it is I project, but it's rare for me to be anywhere where there are prophetic people and not get a word from God. During my season at Bethel, I continued to receive the same prophetic words I had received since 1990.

From all the words, past and present, some things were very clear to me. I'm called to be a mother to nations. I'm called to teach and preach the gospel of the Kingdom. I'm called to be a mentor to young people, and Africa is a major key in my destiny. I'm called to teach the young people of Africa the treasures of the Kingdom. I'm called to restore to them the dominion that was lost during colonialism and restore to them the DNA of Kingdom citizenship. Prophecy after prophecy, I began to store up a pile of promises about a brilliant future.

The more prophetic words I got, the more depressed I got. The life God was describing was amazing and I wanted it. I wanted it more than anything. But I was stuck being a doctor. And I had no idea how I was going to become this amazing pioneer, worshipper, teacher, world traveler and everything else He was talking about. I was stuck, trapped, and committed to a life I didn't love. I didn't know how to get from that trapped place to the glorious life God was talking about through everyone with an ounce of a prophetic gift around me.

During my job at Georgia State University, I picked up the manuscript I had started writing back in medical school. Remember the book about the girl that was miserable because she had followed her parents' dreams for her life instead of her own? The story came back in full force and I found great comfort in writing it. It became my therapy. I finished the book and started trying to get a publishing deal.

As I mentioned, my marriage was at its worst then, so I started writing a book about a woman whose marriage completely fell apart and all the emotions that came with that. I kept submitting both books, but couldn't get a deal. I took writing classes, read books about the craft, edited the books over and over, but for four years, I still couldn't get a deal.

My genre was the problem. I was writing Christian fiction, but apparently it wasn't Christian enough. My characters fornicated, drank wine, sometimes cursed, and did stuff that all the Christians I knew actually did. The companies I was submitting to wanted picture perfect characters that never did anything wrong. Since fiction is based on conflict and I wanted to write about real characters having real experiences, I didn't think that was possible. So I kept submitting and kept getting rejection letters and kept perfecting my craft.

Finally, a new publishing company was created – Urban Christian – that was interested in edgy, Christian fiction with real characters that made mistakes but grew and were redeemed in the end. Me and my sistawriterfriends in a writing group I had founded believed the line was started just for us. Yeah, I'm His favorite.

I submitted the second book and hoped and prayed. One day, the email I had been waiting for those FOUR long years finally came. I read the acceptance email from Urban Christian while sitting at my desk in my office in the prison and screamed! My nurse came running, convinced that one of my prisoner patients had attacked me. We danced and praised and laughed that day. I was going to be a published author!

I published my first book, *My Soul Cries Out*, in July of 2007 and published the first book I actually ever wrote about the young woman desperately in search of her purpose, *Dance Into Destiny*, a year later.

During that time, I was working at the prison full time, writing and marketing my books full time, and attending Bethel Atlanta School of Supernatural Ministry as a first year student. I was grinding hard. I barely watched television, hung out with friends less often, and even read fewer books than normal in order to make my dreams come true. I was still dreaming about all the promises God had made me, but was still on the edge of depression, wondering if they would ever come true.

Let me just stop here and say that if you have dreams, you're going to have to sacrifice to make them come true. If you're not willing to do the work, stop dreaming. When you have a dream you want to birth, you have to make it a high priority in your life. Turn off the television, and get rid of other unproductive time wasters. You may also have to take time away from things you enjoy for the sake of your dreams. Focus, partner with God, and work hard to turn your dreams into tangible realities.

I continued to get prophetic words everywhere I went. All about everything God had been saying all along. I told God, "Please, don't give me another prophetic word. You're just making me depressed, talking about this life that I want but can't seem to live."

My heartfelt, frustrated prayer didn't change a thing. The very next time I went to a church service, I got called out. "You there, in the orange shirt. God is saying that you're a worshipper and you're called to take nations."

I know I rolled my eyes.

I had started to hate my job so much that every morning, I woke up filled with sadness and dread. I dreamed of ways to get out of work. Which is a dangerous thing when you're a Christian who can't lie, but you're also a doctor. I knew I could drink syrup of Ipecac, which would make me throw up. If I called and said my stomach was upset and I was vomiting, I wouldn't be lying. Certainly that was enough to get me out of a day or two of work, wasn't it? Yeah, it was that bad.

Finally, in November of that year, right before Thanksgiving break, I kinda snapped. I couldn't imagine the thought of going to work at the prison another day. I felt like if I went to work on Monday, I would go "postal." I would shoot up the place and end up behind bars wearing the orange jumpsuit instead of taking care of the people in the jumpsuits behind bars.

The Saturday before Thanksgiving, I went online and booked a trip to Jamaica. I called my boss and told him I wouldn't be at work the next week. I knew he could sense that things weren't good with me lately, so he quickly agreed.

I took my Bible, plenty of worship music, and my journals and recordings of all my prophetic words. I went to Jamaica alone and sat on the beach and cried out to God. Every day, I read and listened to my prophetic words. I prayed, I cried, I fussed and argued and let God know I was unhappy with my life. I wanted more. I wanted the ever-elusive life He kept promising that I had no clue of how to get to.

I wanted to be a nation taker, a mother of nations, a prophetic worshipper, a teacher, a world traveler, a mentor of African youths. Who wouldn't want that life and to live out those promises?

I went through this ritual for the whole week. I enjoyed my meals and exercised, and enjoyed the beach, but I was mostly preoccupied with getting an answer from God about my life and future. Finally on Thanksgiving Day, I sat on the beach, rehearsing my prophetic words back to God.

"God, You said I was going to be a mother of nations. You said I was going to preach in stadiums. You said I was going to lead worship and bring down heaven. You said I was going to mentor young people in Africa. God, You said…"

I rehearsed all His promises back to Him. I have to admit it wasn't a sweet conversation on my part. I was bitter and angry and hurt and depressed. I felt unheard and unseen by Him. I was tired of waiting on His promises. I had even started to wonder whether the promises He'd made were just pipe dreams.

I cried and prayed and ranted and finally came to the point where I said – almost shouting on the empty beach – "God, when are you going to make good on all the promises you've made me?!"

His sweet, loving, calm voice – clear as day – answered me, ***"When are YOU going to do all the things I've told you."***

I was completely confused and bewildered. "I'm waiting on YOU!" I replied. I thought for a second and pointed to my chest. "You're waiting on me?"

I could feel Him nodding and smiling. I sat there confused. I had been waiting on God for years to launch me into this destiny He had been promising. How could it be that He was waiting on me? I sat there, processing and taking it in.

I finally asked, "Okay, what do you want me to do?"

Again, clear as day, ***"Quit your job."***

"Huh?" Insert blank stare emoji here… "Quit my job? What?"

He said it again, clearly, ***"Quit your job."***

I nodded, relieved but terrified. "Okay, and then what?"

"Quit your job and then I'll tell you."

"Oh no, God, we ain't playing that Abraham stuff. Leave your house and then I'll tell you where to go. You know me better than that. I need answers."

He simply smiled. ***"Quit your job and then I'll tell you what to do next."***

I sat there quiet again, listening to the waves crashing against the shore. I love the beach. I love staring out over the horizon, in wonder at the awesomeness of God. He always speaks to me at the beach and as I look at the powerful expanse of the ocean, I always know that He's in perfect control.

"You can trust me. I got you."

I said back to Him. "Okay, you're asking me to take a huge leap. I'm gonna jump, but if I do...when I do, you better catch me."

He laughed and smiled. He's such a sweet Father. I felt His peace. I was going to quit my job. I had absolutely no idea what I would do next, but I knew He did. And that was enough for me.

Five

Okay, so maybe it wasn't enough. When I got back to Atlanta, the magic of our sweet, intimate time on the beach wore off and reality hit. Quit my job? And live how? I had a mortgage. I had paid off all my other debts while hoping for God's promises to be fulfilled. I had paid off my student loans, my car and everything. I had saved enough money to live on for two years. I was ready. But I didn't know for what. He wasn't giving any information past quitting my job.

So I got back and December came and went and I didn't quit. I reasoned that I had been emotional on that beach. God hadn't really spoken. I was tired and depressed and wanted out of medicine. But God wasn't crazy. He was rational and wise. And surely He wouldn't expect me to quit my job when I had no plan.

I continued to work. Continued to be miserable and depressed. Continued to hope for the life He had promised.

I always take my birthday off. On that January 13th, I sat in my prayer room and prayed and cried again, pretty much like I had on the beach. I whined and cried and rehearsed His promises and threw a pretty good tantrum, expressing my misery. I went on and on for a while.

And then I heard Him. ***"I told you to quit your job."***

His voice was so clear, I jumped and looked around the room. My heart pounded in my chest. After taking a few deep breaths, I engaged His presence. "Oh, that really WAS You on the beach." I sat for a second to let it sink in. God meant for me to quit my job. He really expected me to quit. And me whining and begging wasn't going to make His answer any different.

I let out a deep breath. "I guess there's no point in me asking what's next. Okay, God. I'll quit. Again, when I jump, you better catch me. Okay?" I felt the same peace I had felt on the beach that day.

The next day, I walked into my boss's office and in fear and trembling resigned my job – and my life – as a doctor.

My dad thought I was crazy. My mom was excited that I was finally going to live my dreams. Daddy tried to talk me out of it, especially since I didn't have a plan. But I wasn't to be moved. I was SURE I had heard God on the beach and in my prayer room. I didn't know what He had in store, but I knew *Him*. And this time, that really was enough.

I had to work one whole month before I could leave. That was one of the longest months of my life. I wanted it to hurry up and be over, but then I didn't know what I was supposed to do next. Every day, I asked Him what was next. And every day, He just smiled and said He would show me when it was time.

On the very last day at work, I got an email from a young lady in Cameroon. She had read *Dance into Destiny* and said it moved her heart. The youth group in the book reminded her of her youth group in Cameroon. The characters' struggle with living in destiny reminded her of her own personal struggle.

I got letters from readers all the time, but for some reason, this one rocked me to my core. A young woman in Africa could totally relate to my characters? It ministered to her and she wanted to know more about how to live in purpose and destiny?

I took a few days and wrote her back. We started corresponding, slowly at first and then eventually daily. I loved learning about her life in Africa and loved pouring into her in her quest for destiny.

Soon after we started chatting, I started waking up at odd hours – one, two, three in the morning, crying out to God in intercession for the nation of Cameroon. I didn't know much about the country. My mom had gone there about sixteen years before as a Fulbright Scholar so I knew a little, but not enough that I should be waking up praying.

God showed me the country in revival. I saw it covered in His glory and majesty and affecting the nations around it. The prayers were seriously disturbing my sleep and therefore my busy life.

I told my new Cameroonian friend, Mimi, about the late night/early morning intercession. She sent me an LOL and said that she and her entire youth group were praying for me to come over and preach at their 7th anniversary in July. I agreed to buy a ticket and come over to minister if they would stop praying and let me sleep!

And so I did. I bought a ticket to go to Cameroon to stay with a person I'd only met over the Internet and minister to a group I'd only heard of through her. Every time I think back on it, it sounds completely crazy, but at the time, it made perfect sense.

I sent her a box of books – my novels and various books from Bethel Church authors. She and the members of her youth group were so excited and devoured them. They couldn't wait for my visit and I couldn't wait to go.

Around that time, I released my third book, *The List*. I still had no idea what I was supposed to be doing. I was speaking and visiting book clubs and selling my books, but it definitely wasn't enough money to live on. I had quit my job like God had told me to, but He still hadn't made good on His end of the bargain to give me instructions as to what to do next.

So why not a mission trip to Africa? I had been to Jamaica and Barbados with Apostle Peterson and loved both trips. But this was my opportunity to fulfill my prophetic word about Africa.

About a month before I was to leave, my dad went for elective surgery to have a precancerous polyp removed from his colon. The surgery went well, but a few days after, he had more pain than he should have. I went on a ministry trip to South Carolina. On my way back, I got a call that they discovered my dad's bowel was perforated and he had to go in for emergency surgery to repair it.

Being a doctor, I realized that was serious and life threatening. It was a difficult, four-hour drive to get to the hospital. When I arrived, the surgeons were leaving, saying everything had gone well. I was relieved. I had spent the whole drive praying and shaking with a sense of foreboding for nothing. Daddy was fine.

When the anesthesiologists came out, their faces spoke a different story than what the surgeons had given. They reported that they couldn't keep my dad's blood pressure stable. His heart rate was elevated and something was wrong. We went to his bedside in the small ICU and he looked awful. Thankfully, after years of having traumatic memories from that night, I can hardly remember the exact details.

I do remember that his blood pressure dropped to the point where the monitor read XX/XX – meaning he had no registerable blood pressure. His heart rate was still there – thank God he never flat lined – but his heart was racing trying to keep blood perfusing his body.

They started transfusing him, liter after liter after liter. They put a blood pressure cuff around the liters of blood and pumped it up for the high pressure to force the blood in. At the same time, they were filling him with liter after liter of fluid. This went on for hours, with him having a very low or no registered blood pressure. Me and mom realized that Daddy was on the verge of death and called my sisters to come in.

We called our pastors and a friend from Bethel Atlanta, who had seen many miracles in his short history as a Christian. They all came and we gathered around the bed. I'm not sure how that worked in the cramped ICU room full of nurses pumping in blood and fluids and the anesthesiologist trying to monitor the situation.

My dad started swelling really badly from the fast infusion of all the fluids. He started to look like the Michelin tire man. Even the whites of his eyes were swollen to the point where he couldn't shut them.

We all prayed fervently. I repeated my dad's prophetic words over his life to him. I stood shaking at the head of the bed, whispering in his ear, "You can't die. God has said you're supposed to mentor young men and lead them to a standard of Christianity and manhood. You can't die because you haven't fulfilled the word that you're going to serve as a father to men of God. You can't die because..." I rehearsed every prophetic word over my father's life that I knew of.

I will never forget the moment where I looked up at the monitor, registering that deadly XX/XX and my dad lifted his hands and croaked out the words in a loud, fierce, whisper, "Let me go...let me go...let me go..."

I stopped whispering in his ear, and started yelling. "No, you can't die. I release the Kingdom and I release life. I command the Kingdom of God to enter this room and chase away death. You shall not die, but live and you'll fulfill every promise God has spoken over your life. I rebuke death in the name of Jesus and command it to go. You will not take my father. I command you to get out of this room." I wasn't praying soft and sweet. I didn't care about the doctors and the nurses. I refused to let my father go and I felt all of heaven backing me.

I started shivering and speaking in tongues uncontrollably. I kept proclaiming life and releasing the Kingdom and the glory of God all over my dad. This was at about two in the morning. We were all praying loud and hard, not caring that we were in an ICU – me, my first year BASSM pastor, Tracy Cooper and her husband Steve, my pastor's wife, Lindy and newly saved, radical revivalist, Drew Kaiser. They had driven more than an hour at about one in the morning to come war for my father's life with us.

It seemed like forever, but the surgeons finally showed up and decided that my dad must have some internal bleeding from the surgery the night before. They took him back to the OR, still with barely any blood pressure, still being transfused with blood and flooded with fluids.

Those were most definitely the longest few hours of my life. I couldn't shut my doctor brain off. The adrenaline and the anointing from praying had lifted and I sat in that hospital room in stark fear, waiting for the surgeons to come back and tell us they had lost my father on the table.

Me, my mom, and sisters made light conversation with our Bethel Atlanta family (Mom was in the first year of BASSM with me.). I kept thanking them for coming to pray. I was amazed that these people I'd known for a little over a year had shown up in the wee hours of the morning, an hour from their home and they were waiting and praying with us.

The surgeons finally came into the room at about five in the morning with grave looks on their faces. They started apologizing and my heart was seized with panic. They had found that in repairing the colon, they had nicked the pancreatic artery. Daddy had hemorrhaged into his belly and that's why no matter how much blood they poured in, he still wasn't able to maintain a blood pressure. It was pouring out as fast as they were pouring it in. I kept waiting for them to say it. With the looks on their faces, the apologetic tone to their voices, and the serious tension in the atmosphere – surely Daddy was gone…

But then they said, "We were able to repair it. The bleeding has stopped and his blood pressure is now stable."

I gasped out the words, "You mean he's alive?"

The surgeon frowned and nodded, like he couldn't understand why I was surprised. "Yes, he's stable, but unconscious. You'll be able to see him soon."

I screamed, "You should have said that first!" and slid down the wall in a heap of tears.

I couldn't believe he had survived it. Even though we had been prophesying and proclaiming life around his bed the whole evening. Sorry, God…

Needless to say there was a lot of praise and thanksgiving in that room. I knew our prayers and prophetic declarations had reached heaven and released angels to preserve Daddy's life. Daddy later told the story that in that moment when he was whispering, "Let me go," he had seen the glory of God. He was headed into heaven and was seeing how glorious it was. He wanted us to stop praying so he could stay forever in the amazing glory he was experiencing.

I'll detour here for a short minute to say that we saints don't realize how much authority we have.

We don't realize that healing power is in our mouths. We literally rebuked death and made it leave. My father was standing at the entryway to heaven, begging us to stop praying so he could go in. He says it all disappeared and he was brought back. He actually gets a tear in his eye every time he tries to find words to explain how glorious that moment was. Right after the tear falls, he gets a tiny bit of an attitude with us for bringing him back. Like we kept him out of heaven. But then he tells us how much he loves us and is glad he stayed with us.

What if we didn't know our authority? What if we accepted the medical facts and stood there and watched him die? What if we didn't know we could rebuke death and release the Kingdom and life over my father?

Thank God for my church family who came to stand with us that night, at great inconvenience to them and their families. There's nothing like Kingdom family that knows the power of Kingdom authority. If it weren't for us standing in the room that night, fighting for my father's life, this would be the end of the book. Or there wouldn't have been a book because of the sad ending. I know the enemy tried to end, or at least severely delay my purpose and destiny that night, but God didn't allow it. Or maybe *we* didn't allow it. It's a lot to think about.

The hard part wasn't over. My dad was intubated and on life support in that ICU room for ten days. We continued to pray and release the Kingdom in his room and over his body. Every part of him was grotesquely swollen. Can you imagine looking at your dad with a large tube down his throat, being regulated by machines, the whites of his eyes so swollen that they looked like gelatinous pools peeking out from under his swollen eyelids?

But the peace of God was there. The day after the crisis, my pastor came. I tried to prepare him for what he would see when he went into the ICU room, 'cause honestly, Daddy looked pretty gross. But all Pastor Steve Hale did when he came into the room was take a deep breath and say, "Hmmm…it feels good in here."

And it did. Instead of feeling like impending death like most ICU rooms, all you could feel was life, peace, and hope. The anointing from the prayers the night before still lingered. Oh, there's so much about the spiritual realm we don't fully understand.

I'll spare you the details. Daddy had many crises with his blood pressure and with the attempt to wean him off the ventilator. But eventually he woke up. He talked out of his head for a while, but he slowly came back to himself and made sense.

There was a big problem though. He couldn't move his extremities. He could talk and think and recognize everybody, but he couldn't move his arms and legs. The doctors kept telling us to give it time, and he would be fine. We were moved to a large VIP patient room for him to recover. It was the week I was supposed to leave for Cameroon, but my dad was in the hospital. There was no way I was leaving.

After he woke up from those surgeries, Daddy was excessively loving, deep, full of words of profound wisdom, imparting so much to us as a family. He called me to his bedside and told me I was not to cancel my trip to Cameroon. It was God's will for me to go and he believed I had a great work to do there. We weren't going to let the devil stop me from doing God's work.

I was shocked. This was my dad who wasn't in support of me quitting my job with no clear plan. The same guy who didn't understand why I was going to a ministry school and didn't believe in all this speaking in tongues and prophesying stuff. He believed in healing, but not the way we did. We had butted heads through the years about me forsaking the doctrine I had been raised in and plunging into stuff he didn't believe in. The deeper I went in God, the more we seemed to disagree.

He told me this trip was important to my destiny and I had to go. We cried together as he told me to get on the plane and go make him and Daddy God proud.

And so I went. A few days later, after feeding him peaches and yogurt because he still couldn't feed himself, Mom took me to the airport, straight from his hospital room. I kissed his balding head a million times before I left. The only way I was able to tear myself away from him was that Daddy God promised me that he'd be there when I got back. With everything that had happened, I secretly feared my father would die and I would never see him again. God reassured me over and over that my father wasn't going anywhere.

On the way to the airport, Mommy mentioned some concerns. "So what do you know about this Mimi and this Youth Aglow group you're going to? I looked them up on the Internet and couldn't find anything. Are you sure they exist? I mean, you're going over here to meet a girl you've been writing on the Internet. Have you Skyped? Have you actually seen her?"

What she didn't say out loud, but I could hear screaming from her mother heart was, "What if this is a scam? What if you fly all the way over there and get kidnapped? How can you trust that this is really real and really God?"

But she kissed me and put me on the plane, of course, a little more afraid than I had been before. The first hour of the plane ride, I fought fears. Fears that my dad was going to die and fears that I was headed to Africa to get kidnapped and held for ransom. My writer brain kicked in and generated a few horrific stories, in vivid detail, about my kidnapping and Daddy's death.

The Holy Spirit finally stepped in and rescued me from my imagination. *"Everything's going to be fine. Your dad is going to be fine and you're going to be fine. Okay? Trust me. I'm with you."*

I nodded and took some deep, calming breaths. He sat there and His peace gave me peace. I wasn't sure what was about to happen in Cameroon, but as always, I was assured of His presence.

Six

When I arrived in Douala, Cameroon, Mimi and her mom were there to greet me. No kidnappers, no scammers, just my sweet friend that I'd gotten to know over the Internet for the past five months.

I was in Africa…

I had gotten my first prophetic word about Africa in 1992. Seventeen years later, I was setting my feet on African soil for the first time. It was 2009 and God's word was finally coming to pass. It was a crazy, surreal, destiny moment. I can't even describe the emotions playing inside of me.

We took a bumpy, crazy ride (which the Cameroonians refer to as jungle driving) in and out of potholes, through horrible traffic, drivers on the wrong side of the road coming straight at us and unnecessary police stops until we finally arrived, about two hours later, in a quiet, villagy town called Buea, in the Southwest region.

As we pulled into the driveway, I whispered to Mimi that I was exhausted from thirty hours of travel and stinky and sticky from the steamy, hot Douala airport. I told her all I wanted to do was shower and sleep. A panicked look entered her eyes. She led me into the house and a large group of young people filled the entire parlor and dining room.

As I entered, they greeted me with a song that was more than music to my ears. The harmony went all the way to my bones and reverberated on what felt like a cellular level, somewhere inside my DNA. I know that sounds dramatic, but something happened in my heart in that moment while they were singing that changed my life forever.

I greeted each of them with a hug, hoping I didn't stink too bad. They each gave a little bow and greeted me as Aunty Sherri. Mimi had told me that young people in Cameroon greeted "older people" as either Aunty, Uncle, Mami or Pa. No matter how many times I insisted she call me Sherri, she refused, horrified that I could even suggest it.

I sampled the many different dishes they had on the long, dining table. Nothing was familiar except for bread. I spoke a little and they spoke a little and again, it sounds dramatic, but my heart was being touched on a level that can't be explained with words.

After they all left, Mimi showed me how to take a bucket bath. Well, actually she didn't show me. She put a bucket of warm water in the middle of the floor in the bathroom and said, "There you go."

I tried as best as I could not to spill any water on the floor and only used half the water. I honestly didn't feel clean after the 30 hours of travel and Douala heat. When I came out, I apologized for getting the floor wet. She gave me a funny look. Afterwards, she explained that it's a bathroom, which means exactly that. I was supposed to get water all over the floor. I was supposed to soap up and then pour water over myself until I was clean.

Then she took me out to the pit toilet. I remembered seeing one once when my dad took us to where he grew up in Dumas, Arkansas, but I had never used one. I'll spare you the details of that experience, except to advise, if you ever find yourself in that position, resist the urge to shine your flashlight down that deep, dark hole…

I wish I could share all the beautiful highlights of that first trip to Cameroon. The very first time we got together for a meeting, they sang to me again. Youth Aglow had its own choir that composed its own songs. They put on a mini concert for me and my heart plunged deeper and deeper in love with them and their country.

After they finished singing, I got up to preach. A few minutes after I launched into my message, it started raining – pouring actually. I didn't realize I had flown into Cameroon in the height of rainy season. It felt like a monsoon and the rain was pounding the zinc roof so loud, I had to stop preaching.

The choir quickly got up and started singing again, this time worshipping God with all their hearts. I was convicted. We were in a simple building with a concrete floor, no paint, no ceiling, a zinc roof, no windows, rows of hard, wooden benches and they were singing loud, heartfelt worship to God, over the deafening rain.

I felt so American in that moment. We're so spoiled. We can't stand any inconvenience and I had hardly seen us worship with such passion in our beautiful, well-appointed churches. These people had so little, yet I hadn't in my life seen such pure joy and dedication to God. I know I keep saying it, but in that moment, my heart was forever changed.

I spent the week teaching them Kingdom principles. We did Kingdom Foundations, Understanding the Prophetic, Identity, the Father Heart of God and other favorite teaching topics of mine. The more I got to know them, the more I realized they were indeed like the youth group in my book, *Dance Into Destiny*. They loved to dance, sing, act, and do anything that had to do with the arts. They loved chasing after God. They were younger versions of me, full of songs, plays, choreography and in love with God's presence and hungry for so much more.

I called Yvette to tell her everything that was happening and she said, "It's like you're caught up in some kind of God vortex. How did you find these people that are just like you and just like what we always dreamed of? In Cameroon? God is crazy!"

I loved the food, the music, the dances, the sense of community, the sleepy quietness of the beautiful, little, villagy town. The trip seemed magical.

Until one day, I got into the bathroom to take a bucket bath to get ready for church and Mimi knocked on the door. I told her I'd be out in a minute, but she said, "It's your mom. About your dad."

I panicked. I counted in my head and realized that it was about three in the morning in Atlanta. If she was up and calling, it couldn't be good.

My heart dropped as she shared the latest news. A blood vessel had burst in Daddy's head. The CT showed a large bleed so much so that his brain had shifted. My doctor brain knew what that meant. He had only a 30% chance of living and even if he did survive, he wouldn't be a brilliant doctor anymore. He'd be a vegetable.

They were transferring Daddy to Emory Hospital for emergency brain surgery. Emergency neurosurgery. Ambulance to Emory for emergency surgery to drain the blood off his brain. The words barely made sense.

I dried off and got dressed and explained to Mimi what was happening. She simply said, "We'll pray with the others when we get to church."

When we get to church? Didn't she just hear me say my dad was probably about to die or at least become a vegetable? I argued that I didn't want to go to church. I couldn't preach that morning. What in the world was she thinking?

She asked me, "What can you do about it? You're here. Might as well preach."

So I got dressed and we went to church. I told the kids what was going on and asked them to pray. They warred for my father's life. They prayed, sang, worshipped, prophesied and declared life over him – as if he were their own father. The same kind of radical love poured out by my Bethel Atlanta family was being poured out by this group of young radicals I had just met. I was overwhelmed.

We stopped for a lunch break and I called mom. She said dad had come through surgery just fine. They were able to remove all the blood. Dad was stable. I remembered the ten days on life support he had just come through and fearfully asked the question, "When can they take the tube out?"

"It's already out. God is good, Sherri. You and those kids keep praying."

Needless to say, part two of our church meeting was a downright celebration. We praised and danced and sang as only Africans can. And I fell more in love with this little country named Cameroon and its beautiful people.

I was supposed to meet my sweet friend and fellow BASSM year one grad, Grace Davis, in Mozambique to meet my missionary shero, Heidi Baker and stay at her mission base in Pemba for a while. But clearly, I had to get home to see my father. Mom tried desperately to change my ticket, but I couldn't get out of Cameroon any sooner than originally planned. So I stayed and preached and imparted and poured into Youth Aglow until it was time to leave. I adopted Mimi's philosophy. I was there, so I might as well minister.

I received much more than I had poured out on that visit to Cameroon and I knew I would never be the same. I didn't realize I had been bit by the missionary bug and had contracted an incurable disease – missions for life. I stored up the amazing experiences in my heart and prepared myself for the long journey home.

I had left for Cameroon straight from my father's hospital room to the airport and now I was returning, straight from the airport to his room in the Neuro ICU at Emory. My mom had been pretty vague about things while I was in Cameroon, reassuring me that Daddy was fine and was recovering well. In the car on the way to the hospital though, the truth started coming out. His blood pressure was fluctuating. He'd had a seizure the day before and had actually asked them to hurry and get me home because he was afraid he would never get to see me again.

I will never forget walking into his room that day. The whole right side of his head was wrapped in a huge bandage and his left eye was literally bulging out of his head in a scary, freaky, ominous way. I was horrified at how much my mom had protected me from.

She had a huge, tired and slightly zany smile on her face when she patted his cheek and looked up at me and said, "Doesn't he look great?"

No, Mom, he doesn't look great. He looks like death warmed over. Do you not see his eye bulging out of his head?

But she had been through hell and back while I was gallivanting and living my dreams in Cameroon, so I said, "He looks great, Mommy. God is good."

I won't prolong the story. My dad went through a long rehab process at Emory. He was finally transferred to their rehab hospital because he still couldn't walk. He worked hard with the physical and occupational therapists.

Things were going well enough, but we were concerned that he had lost something. My dad can answer any question about anything. I always ask him, "How do you know that? WHY do you know that?" when he gives a brilliant, factual answer. My dad, who could rival Google, couldn't recognize a crossword puzzle, even though he'd worked them for years. He couldn't solve a Sudoku puzzle or answer a complicated question.

We finally brought him home after a nightmarish, 77-day hospital stay. We had the house outfitted for his wheelchair and he moved into the bedroom on the first floor. A few friends helped lift his wheelchair up the front steps to the house because the ramp wasn't ready yet. We wheeled him into that first floor bedroom and they helped us transfer him to the bed. Me, my mom, and sisters gathered around him in the bed with hugs, kisses, and many tears. He couldn't walk, his brain wasn't as sharp, but he was alive. And he was *home*.

We hired a home health nurse to come take care of him. The first time I met her, I instantly recognized her accent. I asked and she confirmed that she was Cameroonian. I told her I had just come back from a great mission trip to her country. She said she had a brother who was a missionary, too. He had lived in America for a while, but had moved his family back to Cameroon to do ministry there. I gave her my information for him to contact me, but didn't think much of it.

Dad's care was intense. He couldn't walk or do much of anything for himself. Me and Mom poured a lot of time and love into caring for him. It was unsettling to see my dad, who usually power-walked five to seven miles a day, played golf several times a week, and drove himself everywhere stuck in a wheelchair. We were thankful he was alive, but it was a huge adjustment to a new normal.

Dad came to Bethel Atlanta one Sunday to tell about his miraculous healing and to thank Bethel Atlanta for their prayers the times he almost died. He sat through worship and the other healing testimonies. We wheeled him to the front so he could give his testimony.

When he finished, he said, "Well, God has been real good. He's saved my life and healed me. And because of that, I think I'm gonna get up out of this chair and walk back to my seat."

And he did.

My dad stood and took his first unaided steps – after four surgeries, two on-the-edge-of-death episodes, a ruptured blood vessel in his brain, paralysis of his extremities, severe fluid on the lungs, and bacteria in his blood – back to his seat.

Me, mom and my older sister lost it and fell apart with tears of joy. The whole church erupted in praise. I'm not sure how we got it back together to finish service that day. My dad was healed. He had lived and not died and now, in an instant, he could walk! We were all high on the goodness of God.

As my dad's condition continued to improve and he started to regain all his faculties – started driving and working Sudoku puzzles and answering every question under the sun, I started getting restless. The missions virus was multiplying in my blood and I was itching to get back to Cameroon.

I was well into my second year at BASSM and loving every minute of it. As they were planning their mission trips, I planned another trip to Cameroon. I had just left Cameroon in July and in November, I found myself on a plane, going again. This time I took radical revivalist, Drew Kaiser, who had helped pray my dad back to life that night at the hospital.

I stayed for three weeks that time and poured into "my kids" all the more. They were hungry for more of God and I was hungry to teach them. Drew led them on hospital outreaches and we saw many miracles. One older gentleman had been paralyzed and bedridden for about a month. Drew and some of the kids prayed for him and they came back to us with a video of the man dancing and praising God all around the hospital ward. The more miracles we saw, the hungrier we became for more miracles.

God started talking crazy stuff to me personally in my times of morning prayer. I don't honestly remember when the thought first entered my mind. What if I start a Bethel Atlanta School of Supernatural Ministry here in Cameroon? I know now that God must have planted that thought as a seed. Where else would it have come from? I had to be honest, though. I enjoyed my short mission trips to Cameroon, but I didn't think I could live there long term.

I had to take bucket baths because there was no running, hot water. It was either freezing cold showers or hot water in a bucket. The mattresses were made of foam and not long after lying down, I could feel my body sinking and sinking until it was pressed into the bed's wood slats. I'm like the princess and the pea when it comes to my sleep and I never got a good, deep sleep while in Cameroon. I'd been sleeping on pillow-top mattress for years and the foam seemed like an insult to my body.

And we had to walk a lot. I've always power-walked three to four miles a day for exercise, but we weren't on sidewalks or nicely paved trails. This was on dirt roads with jagged rocks, and thick mud or a carpet of dust depending on whether it was rainy or dry season. We passed chickens and goats and there was one particular steep, rocky hill that Mimi practically skipped her way up, but I had to place my hand on the ground just to keep my balance. I always wondered how many chickens and goats had passed and pooped there.

One day, we were headed up the hill and I came face to face with a huge pig. I freaked out, but Mimi only laughed and asked me why I was afraid of a small pig.

We had to go to Internet cafés just for me to stay in contact with my family and the Internet was painfully slow. Painfully. There wasn't running water 24/7 and there were frequent power outages or low voltage where the electricity was there, but barely, so you'd be sitting in a room squinting because the lights were so dim.

There was no Starbucks decaf soy latte, no movie theatres, no spa pedicures, no international restaurants, no spring mix salads with salmon and goat cheese, no cute coffee shops with ambiance where I could write or just daydream, no place to listen to live jazz, no Mommy hugs. I couldn't rub my Daddy's head, no all-day plotting sessions with me and Yvette figuring out how we were going to take over the world, no ATL vibe – none of the things I had grown to deeply love about my life.

Nowhere was comfortable. The beds were thin foam on hard wood. The chairs and couches were thin cushions on hard wood. You may think I sound like a spoiled American, but come stay a week in Cameroon – not in my apartment or our guesthouse – and see how many things you don't even realize you take for granted.

I loved the high of a two or three week visit to Cameroon, but wasn't sure this diva could handle living there long term.

I returned home with a dream of starting a BASSM in my heart, competing with reluctance about living in Cameroon. I knew Bethel Church had a BSSM DVD curriculum, so I decided I would send the DVD's over and then visit twice a year for impartation. It sounded like a perfect plan that would fulfill my prophetic words about pouring into young people in Africa.

Not too long after I got back, Eric Johnson, Bill Johnson's son, came to Bethel Atlanta to minister in the church and at BASSM. I got a few moments alone with him and told him I was excited about starting a DVD school in Cameroon. His answer was clear, concise and pierced my heart.

He thought it was an amazing idea for me to take BASSM to Cameroon. From his experience, the

DVD schools were great, but the schools with the most success were the ones where someone who carried the Bethel DNA was there, on the ground, pouring into the people. He looked me straight in my eyes, gave me a big smile, patted me on the shoulder and walked away, leaving me there with my mouth open.

It was one of those undeniable God moments. I felt the Holy Spirit standing there smiling and nodding, as if He was agreeing with Eric's words.

If I wanted the school to be as successful as possible, I needed to go to Cameroon. I needed to move to Cameroon. I needed to be in Cameroon long term.

Oh God, I was challenged...

The next week at BASSM, we had one of those crazy-awesome-overwhelming worship nights and I ended up snotting and crying on my knees and saying, "I'll do anything for You, God. I surrender my whole life. I give You everything." I screamed and cried, "Yes, yes, God, yes," over and over until I had no strength. I laughed at myself afterwards. I knew He was going to hold me to it.

I started making plans to move to Cameroon.

Seven

A tug of war went on in my soul over such a huge decision. It makes me giggle inside when people talk about how brave and adventurous I am. If you could have cut my soul open and seen the continuous turmoil, you wouldn't think me so brave and adventurous.

I could swing from an excited high to a scared, nervous low within minutes. I made plans for hours – plotting curriculum and finances and the logistics of moving and then for the next few hours, felt like I had completely lost my mind. I'm no braver than anyone reading this book. I'm just foolishly and helplessly in love with God. His love makes me crazy and I'd do anything He asks.

During those times of struggle, God reminded me of how this cry for revival started in my heart around 1998. When I moved to South Carolina, on one of me and Yvette's God chasing trips to Morningstar Ministries, I bought a book by Rick Joyner called *The Final Quest*. It radically changed my perspective on Christianity. I devoured that book and many others about the moves of God in history and began to feel like I had a part to play in bringing about a worldwide revival.

One day, I sat on my couch reading a book about the Brownsville Revival in Pensacola, Florida. I started crying uncontrollably. There are times when the words we're reading or listening to seem to bypass our mind and go straight to our spirit. I'm pretty sure that's what happened that day because I didn't even know why I was crying.

I'd stop for a few seconds, try to get myself together and then burst into tears all over again. I stopped myself once and said, "What in the world is this? Why am I crying?" No sooner than I had wiped my face and blown my nose, the tears erupted again. This went on for an hour or more, me sobbing uncontrollably for no identifiable reason.

Finally after the tears came deep, guttural prayers – crying out for revival in the nations. I prayed that Jesus would be crowned King over all the earth and finally receive the reward He paid for 2000 years ago, that His government would be established in every nation, tribe, and tongue. I cried out for the unsaved that had never experienced His love and goodness. I cried out for nations that are so overcome with prosperity that they think they don't need Him. I cried out for the millions of people that have never heard His name and don't even know He exists.

I can't remember all the prayers I prayed and some of them were beyond my understanding. I prayed for hours on my living room floor. After crying out for the nations, I began offering my life. I told Him I'd go anywhere, I'd do anything – just give me the honor and privilege of being a part of this revival, no matter the role. I prayed for Him to fill me with the gifts, the strength, the courage, and the love to lay down my life for His Kingdom to be established on Earth.

I was seeking God at the time, hungry for more of Him, but it was Him – my best Friend, His precious Holy Spirit – who guided me into praying the prayers that would pull me into His perfect will for my life.

Looking back, I know that time of prayer and many others like it had been stored up in heaven. It was beginning to feel like now was the time for those prayers to be answered. They weren't emotional moments of surrender in God's presence. They were seeds of intercession sown toward my future.

I'll divert here for a moment to say, so many people worry about finding "the will of God." They sit paralyzed for years, waiting to discover God's plan. Just discover Him! Fall in love with Him and His presence and making His Kingdom a reality on Earth and I promise, He'll get you to where you're supposed to be. He wants you to live purpose and destiny more than you do, so just give Him your heart and trust Him to the make the rest happen.

My favorite book on the topic is *Dreaming With God*, by Bill Johnson. It'll change your whole perspective on finding God's perfect will for your life.

If you're on a quest for purpose and destiny, it's a must read.

As I continued praying about starting a BASSM in Cameroon, I needed help to overcome the doubts and fears that kept creeping up. I asked God for more confirmation. I lived in a prophetic community at Bethel Atlanta and I asked God for some prophetic words that would make it clear. The difficult thing about getting confirmation in the Bethel culture is that we're not allowed to give specific, directional words. Somebody might say, "I see you going to the nations," or "I see you becoming a missionary and ministering to the poor," but that's about it. Nobody could say, "Go to Africa."

I decided to let that be God's problem. I told Him, "You know I'll do anything You ask me to do, but I need to be sure. Half of the time this feels crazy. Ridiculous and crazy. I need You to do whatever You know I need for my heart to be absolutely sure."

No prayer for hours, just a simple conversation with Daddy God. *Make me sure.*

And He did. I went to the yearly Bill Johnson conference in Webb, Alabama. If I could dig out the right journal, I could remember the sermon he preached that had me weeping on the floor, crying out yet another "yes." A messy, snotty, red-faced, surrendered, "I'll go wherever You send me and I'll do whatever You ask," came from the depths of me and I couldn't take it back if I wanted to.

As always, I got called out by members of his team and got a prophetic word about going to the nations. In the lobby, I got a prophetic word while hanging out with some of my fellow BASSM students after the conference was over for the night. It was the precise confirmation I needed. The person saw me in a scene with a setting like *The Lion King*, standing at the top of a mountain overlooking a great valley filled with warriors. I was raising up these young warriors to be revivalists and we were marching across the nations bringing transformation everywhere we went.

My heart nearly exploded in my chest. It was just like a scene in one of the Rick Joyner books. Almost an exact description. After reading it, I had prayed to raise up a mighty army of revivalists to bring Kingdom transformation to the nations. The same prayer I had prayed was coming back to me in a prophetic word, many years later. I love *The Lion King* and thought it was clever of God to sneak me a directional word that way.

Several more prophetic words came that weekend. I was finally sure. After that time, I never looked back. I'm an obsessive-compulsive planner and from that moment, I went after it. All roads led to Cameroon.

I can't say enough about the importance of being a part of a prophetic community. That simply means being around a bunch of people who value the voice of God in their lives. For years, I've surrounded myself with people who have the ability to hear God and it's a high core value in our lives. We hear God for ourselves and for our own big decisions and we endeavor to hear God for each other.

For me, there's so much safety in that. I rarely make any big moves that aren't confirmed, "...out of the mouth of two or three witnesses." Sometimes, the prophetic words are a confirmation of something I'm already thinking and praying about. Other times, God presents a new idea through another person that I may have never thought of on my own.

It's not like we're being deep and spooky and sitting prophesying to each other wearing long, John the Baptist robes and serious looks on our faces. This happens when we're out to dinner and talking about life around the table. I may be in morning prayer and someone's face pops into my head and God gives me a word for them.

It's about living in tune with God and always being ready to receive from Him. I'm sure I'll write a book on the prophetic and "living by His whispers" one day soon, so I won't go too much deeper into this topic. I'll finish by saying this – my life is an amazing, extravagant adventure because I value hearing the Father's voice through my intimate relationship with Him and through relationship with others who hear His voice. I don't understand how people live life successfully without the prophetic and without prophetic community.

During this huge transition period, God sat down with me in my prayer room one day. I was excited about the upcoming move, but still somewhat dreading the drastic change in lifestyle.

He asked me, *"**What would make this easier for you?**"*

I was so touched that He cared. It wasn't just about me sacrificing to do His will. He cared about how I felt and wanted me to be happy and not just obedient. Just in case you missed it, I'll say it again – God has a call for my life, but He actually cares about how I feel. He wants me to be happy and fulfilled and not just obedient.

As I mentioned at the beginning, I think that's a huge reason why people don't lay down their lives to God completely. We're afraid of what it will cost us. When we think of serving God fully, we think of sacrifice, hardship, pain, suffering, until we finally die and go to heaven. I won't get too far ahead of myself and will just say, nothing could be further from the truth. God wants us to live life abundantly (John 10:10). He wants us to enjoy life.

I've noticed in my Bethel Atlanta Cameroon staff that people work the hardest and are the most productive when they love what they do. I watch and ask probing questions to learn the hearts of my staff. What do they dream about? What are they called to? What would give them the most fulfillment? And then I try to adjust things to put them in a position where the dreams of their heart are answered. And they are the most devoted, hard-working, loyal staff. Why? Because I care about their hearts and push them to live their dreams. I put them in positions where they get to do what they were born to do. My heart's desire is for them to feel happy and fulfilled.

If I'm smart enough to do that, wouldn't God be even smarter? He could put me somewhere that I hate where I'm unhappy and unfulfilled and I would do my best because He's God. But He wouldn't get the absolute best out of me. But if He puts me in a place that makes my DNA vibrate with a feeling of home and lets me do exactly what I've always dreamed of doing since childhood, I'll pour out my life, simply because I love it. Not only because I love Him.

So we sat on the chaise that day, trying to figure out what made me think life in Cameroon was going to be so hard. The first thing I brought up was the foam bed situation.

"Sorry for being such a princess, but You know how I am when I don't get a good night's sleep."

He laughed and nodded. ***"Yeah, I do. What else?"***

I eased into the conversation more, realizing that He wasn't irritated by my being such a spoiled brat diva. "I know this sounds silly, but the chairs are hard. In fact, the whole place feels hard and uncomfortable."

I could see the love in His eyes and hear it in His voice. ***"I don't think that's silly at all. But that's an easy fix. Ship your furniture."***

The thought had never occurred to me. I could ship my pillow-top mattress and my brown, leather couch and my favorite, red, leather chair?

"Okay, what else?"

His care for me was overwhelming. I thought for a minute more. "I don't know if I can do bucket baths long term. I know it's a small thing, but I really love hot showers."

"Okay, when you chat with Mimi again, ask about a hot water heater."

Duh…okay. Why didn't I think of that? We continued to run down the list of issues and He kept coming up with easy fixes until I felt…better.

We have such a loving, good Father who cares about our hearts. He's concerned about the little things. Every little and big detail of our life matters to Him. More of us would lay down our lives completely if we truly knew that. By the time we finished talking, I felt a lot more peace about my move to Cameroon. The peace that comes with being intimately known and deeply loved.

Me and Mimi chatted almost every day planning out every detail we could. It was her task to help me find somewhere to live and a building for the school. I made plans for the curriculum and did some budgeting – as much budgeting as you can do when you're living "by faith" on donations and don't know how much money will be coming in.

Mimi started looking for the building for us to hold classes in. We didn't know how many students to anticipate, so we weren't sure of the type of building we should be looking for. We chatted endlessly – planning, dreaming, and deciding – doing everything we knew to start the school.

After a while, it seemed like every time I chatted with Mimi, something was going wrong. She had found a building that was large and centrally located – perfect for the school. We started planning everything with that building in mind, but then the deal fell through and we were back to nothing.

Mimi was then diagnosed with resistant malaria and was admitted to the hospital to receive a slew of IV medications to treat it. She asked me to pray for her, not knowing how scary it was for me, realizing I was moving to a country where I could get a killer disease from a simple mosquito bite.

There were spiritual attacks on many members of Youth Aglow during that time. In the United States, we don't know much about spiritual attacks. We aren't often exposed to witchcraft and demonic oppression/possession, so when Mimi described what was going on, I was like, "Where in the world am I moving to???"

One of the Youth Aglow members was being tormented to the point that it was affecting her mind.

As things worsened, they had to take her to a church and tie her up to keep her from harming herself or others. A few of the members stayed with her for hours, praying for her and ministering to her physical and spiritual needs, but the situation lasted longer than I thought it should. Weren't we supposed to be able to cast out demons with a word?

Another of the Youth Aglow young women took care of the tormented woman into the wee hours of the morning. On her way home, she was robbed and almost raped. She fought and begged the guy until he finally ran off.

Mimi kept sending me prayer requests about all these issues, thinking she was appealing to some great, spiritual leader, full of faith and miracles. I was like, "Malaria, demons, and robbers? God, are you sure I'm supposed to move there?"

To be completely honest, I freaked out. Even though God had bent over backwards with prophetic word after prophetic word and had given me peace and assurance that this was His destiny for me, at the first sign of trouble, I was ready to bail.

I did what I've learned to do and got really still so we could have a serious talk. I knew the enemy was trying to scare me off and I needed to hear God's heart on the matter. Again...

I was like, "God, there's crazy stuff going on in Cameroon. I'm scared. Is this really you? Are you really gonna take care of me? Am I really supposed to move there?"

His answer changed my life and is the reason for the title of this book. I know it sounds funny, because everything that led up to that point was so miraculous, but it seems like that's when the miracles really started. I'll get to the miracles in a minute. Let me explain the God Zone first.

Eight

In the middle of my freak out, run away from destiny moment, God answered me. His answer has become one of my life messages that I teach every year in the school and often teach when asked to speak about purpose and destiny.

He led me to a Scripture that has become one of my favorites. In Isaiah 9:6-7, there's an amazing Messianic prophesy about the coming of Jesus Christ.

For unto us a Child is born, unto us a Son is given; and the government shall be upon His shoulder, and His name shall be called Wonderful Counselor, Mighty God, Everlasting Father, Prince of Peace. Of the increase of His government and of peace there shall be no end, upon the throne of David and over His kingdom to order and establish it with judgment and justice, from that time forward, even forever.

That last line is profound, *"The zeal of the Lord of Hosts will perform this."*

God used this verse to speak to me very clearly. He said, ***"Not only am I going to take good care of you. You're about to enter into a God Zone where the zeal of the Lord of Hosts performs everything that pertains to you."***

I was floored. That was a huge promise, far beyond anything I had expected Him to say. The zeal, the passion, the power, and the presence of the God of the armies of heaven were going to be behind everything I did. Whoa...

He kept talking. *This isn't a season where you take your prophetic words and war and fight for them to come to the pass. All I need is for you to come into agreement with Me – you've given Me your yes – and you're about to soar into an amazing adventure where everything you put your hand to, the zeal of the Lord of Hosts will perform.*

That did **everything** for my confidence...

Anybody that knows me well, knows I have three major life messages. One is the message of the Kingdom. Purpose and destiny is the second and the third is intimacy with God. I LOVE to pour out my heart and my life in bringing people into these heavenly realities. The God Zone is the place where the message of the Kingdom and the message of purpose and destiny powerfully collide. Intimacy with God is the foundation and cornerstone of every single message I preach.

There are certain things on God's heart and on His mind that He wants to accomplish in the earth. If you can find out what those things are and find out what your role is in bringing God's heart and desire to Earth, then go after that with all your heart. If you give your life to bringing God's desires for Earth to pass, then you can believe that all of heaven and earth will back you.

Another favorite Scripture is at the end of Isaiah 60. The whole chapter again prophesies the release of God's Kingdom on the earth and how the saints of God will arise to build that Kingdom. The chapter ends with this:

A little one shall become a thousand and a small one a strong nation. I, the Lord, will hasten it in its time (Isaiah 60:22).

There are two ways that prophetic words come to pass. Most prophetic words require us to partner with God. They are dependent. If we don't do our part, the prophetic word doesn't come to pass. For example, if I had gotten all those prophetic words about Cameroon, but never started planning, never devised a curriculum, and never bought that plane ticket, my life as a missionary in Cameroon never would have happened. I would still be sitting in Atlanta, trying to figure out when I was going to live my purpose and destiny.

I believe there are sovereign prophetic words that are critical in God's divine plan for the Earth. Jesus Christ coming to establish His Kingdom and reign on Earth was a non-negotiable fact. It was sovereignly accomplished by the zeal of the Lord of Hosts. It was something the Lord hastened in the proper time. Jesus had to be born, go to the Cross, defeat satan and restore authority and dominion to make it happen. Nothing could stop that and all of heaven was involved in bringing it to pass.

It is His sovereign will, His plan and design for the entire Earth that His Kingdom rules over all. Of the increase of the government of Jesus Christ – of His rule and reign – there shall be no end. Jesus' rule began with His life on Earth and it's to continue until His Kingdom conquers the whole earth. Just like the mustard seed and the small measure of leaven in Jesus' parables, the Kingdom starts small and will continue to grow until the knowledge of the glory of the Lord fills the whole Earth as the waters cover the sea (Habakkuk 2:14).

That's how pervasive the glory of God is supposed to be in the earth. If you want to live in the God Zone, then go after causing the whole earth to be filled with His glory. This is something that God will accomplish sovereignly and will use all the resources of heaven to bring to pass.

If you're searching for purpose and destiny, find it in the Kingdom. If you align your destiny with the Kingdom of God coming to earth, you will have all of heaven backing you! If your purpose and destiny furthers the cause of the Kingdom, then you can be assured that the zeal of the Lord of Hosts will accomplish it.

Let me give some examples in the Scriptures to make this foundational point more clear. God's whole purpose and plan when He created the heavens and the earth was for man to have dominion. I'm sure I'll write a book on understanding the Kingdom, so I'll try to keep things brief so we can stay focused on purpose and destiny. The two are so deeply related though, it bears some explanation.

From the moment Adam and Eve sinned and handed dominion of the earth over to satan, God released a plan to restore dominion back to man. Actually, this happened long before the creation story ever happened, as "Jesus was the Lamb slain from the foundations of the earth" (Rev. 13:8). God knew what Adam and Eve would do and already had a plan prepared.

In Genesis 3:15, the first Messianic prophecy about Jesus defeating satan was spoken. *And I will put enmity between you and the woman, and between your seed and her Seed; He shall bruise your head, and you shall bruise His heel.*

The entire story of the Old Testament is the unfolding of God's masterfully orchestrated plan to bring Jesus to earth. He used men and women, aligned with His Kingdom purpose of bringing Jesus to earth, to bring complete restoration of dominion.

Contrary to popular Christian belief, the Old Testament isn't a collection of stories about a bunch of different people we read to get to know more about God. Well, it is, but it's so much more. It's the story of a family – one family – through whom God fulfilled His Messianic promise about bringing Jesus to earth.

It's a long story of who begat who to finally birth Jesus on earth.

From Adam to Noah to Abraham to Jacob and his sons, all the way to Jesus, everyone is related. The patriarchs became the nation of Israel and it was through this nation that Jesus was born.

We know of many stories in the Bible of people in their God Zone – the place where God moves all of heaven and earth to make His plans for the Kingdom succeed. Most of them were a part of this important family lineage through which Jesus was born. Therefore, it was important to God to provide for, protect, and prosper them so Jesus could come through them to Earth to redeem it.

Look at every story in the Old Testament and you'll realize it's all about the Kingdom. All about Jesus coming to Earth to restore dominion back to man.

Abraham became rich and prosperous so he could begin his legacy as the father of the nation of Israel. His sons continued to grow that prosperity and through his grandson Jacob/Israel, the nation of Israel was born.

His son, Joseph, was sold into slavery by his brothers and ended up in prison, but because of this, he became the second in command to the Pharaoh of Egypt, the ruler of the known world at that time. God used Joseph to preserve the family of Jacob/Israel during a time of famine. Joseph enjoyed the prosperity and influence of being second in command of Egypt (his God Zone), but it was all about the Kingdom – saving Israel from extinction before it even became a nation.

The stories of Moses, Joshua, David, and Solomon tell of their journeys into their God Zones, bringing the people out of slavery into their promised land and then establishing them so that they went from being the nation of Israel to the Kingdom of Israel.

Unfortunately, the Israelites continually sinned until they ended up in captivity to other nations. They were no longer their own Kingdom. Their nation was destroyed and they had to serve other kings in the empires of Assyria, Babylon, Medo-Persia, Greece, and Rome. But even in their captivity, God preserved them as a people through which Jesus, the King of Kings would come.

Daniel was an important leader in the captivity during the rule of the Babylonian Empire. He studied the prophecies of Jeremiah and realized the Israelites were supposed to be released to go back to their land in the seventieth year of their captivity. He began repenting and interceding on behalf of the entire nation for God's word to be fulfilled.

On the first day he started praying, the archangel Michael was released to bring his answer. When you're aligned with the purposes of God for establishing His Kingdom, God will mobilize angelic armies to war in the heavens on your behalf – even up to the chief archangel Michael.

The Israelites were indeed released to go back to their land by the Persian King, Cyrus, as was prophesied by Isaiah 150 years before. Many years later, Nehemiah sent word to ask about how they were doing. He got word that the people were in danger because there was no wall of protection around the city. Walls surrounding a city during that time in history were vital for protection against enemies and Jerusalem was surrounded by enemies.

Nehemiah prayed to the God of heaven and then he spoke to the king. God had given him a position of influence as King Artaxerxes's cupbearer. The king granted his request to go and rebuild the walls of Jerusalem and he was given letters of authority with the king's seal of approval. He was also given letters instructing other nations to provide the raw materials needed to build.

The king gave him authority, provision, and protection in order to carry out God's will for His Kingdom people. When you're in your God Zone, focused on establishing the Kingdom in the earth, you'll have everything you need.

I could continue with stories of people in their God Zones – being placed in positions of influence and power over nations to preserve, protect and further the nation/Kingdom of Israel. Esther is another great example. This young Jewish woman became the wife of the Persian King Ahasueres, to save the Jewish people from destruction.

I think it's clear that when you're in your God Zone, you'll experience the miraculous and have everything you need to establish the Kingdom of God – angelic armies warring for you, authority and influence, provision and abundance, protection and security.

God will make sure you have whatever you need to accomplish His overall purpose of establishing His rule, reign and government on Earth.

The next logical question becomes, "What is God doing in the earth now?" Jesus came to Earth, died and was resurrected and is now sitting at the right hand of God. He took dominion and authority over the earth back from satan and gave it back to man.

All authority in heaven and earth has been given to me. Go and make disciples of all nations (Matt 28:18).

Jesus finished His work on the Cross, but yet, we don't see His dominion established over all the earth. The goal, then, is to enforce the authority and dominion that Jesus won at Calvary. That task is left for us to do. There are numerous Scriptures that show us that this is the next step.

And He shall speak peace to the nations. His dominion shall be from sea to sea; and from the River to the ends of the earth (Zec 9:10).

The kingdoms of this world have become the kingdoms of our Lord and of His Christ, and He shall reign forever and ever (Rev. 11:15).

Then to Him was given dominion and glory and a kingdom, that all peoples, nations, and languages should serve Him. His dominion is an everlasting dominion which shall not pass away, and His kingdom the one which shall not be destroyed (Dan 7:14).

For the earth will be filled with the knowledge of the glory of the Lord, as the waters cover the seas (Hab 2:14).

Arise and shine for your light has come! And the glory of the Lord is risen upon you. For behold the darkness shall cover the earth, and deep darkness the people; But the Lord will arise over you and His glory will be seen upon you. The Gentiles shall come to your light, and kings to the brightness of your rising (Isa 60:1-3).

A whole book could be written on the eschatology of when this is all supposed to happen. I'll simply refer to the Scripture where Jesus says, "Occupy until I come." The term occupy doesn't mean to sit and be still. It means to take over and have dominion. We, as Kingdom citizens, are supposed to take over the nations – disciple and establish God's government and authority in them. If you want to live in the God Zone, find a way to establish His Kingdom on Earth.

When I first started waking up and praying for Cameroon, I knew it and the entire continent of Africa were deeply on God's heart. It is His desire for the reality of the Kingdom to radically affect this continent that has been ravaged by colonialism, war, poverty, corruption, occultism and many other societal ills.

Many times in intercession, I could feel the desire of His heart to bring light to what many have called the "Dark Continent." He desires for the knowledge of the glory of the Lord to fill Africa as the waters cover the seas.

It's time for a Kingdom invasion of the nations of Africa. The more He impressed this upon my heart, the more I understood I was being commissioned and released to do more than start a school. I was being called to bring the Kingdom to a nation – and to begin establishing the reality of the Kingdom of God on a continent. Thinking of this is overwhelming...even now.

And since establishing His Kingdom in Africa is a priority on God's heart, the zeal of the Lord of Hosts is exactly what I began to experience when I began to make plans for my move to Cameroon.

The God Zone is the place where your plans and your entire life are purposed towards the things of God and therefore, God moves all of heaven and earth to make even the impossible happen for you. When you lay down your life for His Kingdom, He takes care of everything – all the details – and your life becomes this supernatural place of provision, favor, divine connections, abundance, etc.

The miracles I've experienced since deciding to give my life completely to God and the advancement of His Kingdom are mind blowing. I get to experience aspects and facets of God's goodness that I never got to experience when I was living the "normal Christian life." When you lay down your life so that His Kingdom can be established, you enter the miraculous God Zone.

That's not to say that you have to move to Africa to further His Kingdom. I'll stress again – that's the call of God on **my** life. The nation you may be called to take might be your family, your neighborhood, your city, the office where you work, your school. The Kingdom needs to be released EVERYWHERE.

In looking back over my life, I can see that I've always lived in the God Zone. I've always enjoyed ridiculous favor and abundance. I have two amazing parents that poured into my life to make me who I am. I got a great education – fully paid for – and was always made to believe I could do anything I put my mind to. I grew up as a church girl, officially saved at the age of eight, but basically born in church. I don't have a "testimony" of any dark period in my life where I was out doing bad stuff and then God radically saved me. Other than my divorce, which ended up being the time that I was drawn into deep intimacy with God, I've lived an amazing, beautiful life.

But when I said yes to Cameroon, the miraculous provision and favor I'd always experienced went to a whole new level.

Nine

The old folks say God helps babies and fools and I feel like my transition to Cameroon testifies to that. If I had stopped for a moment to think of the magnitude of what I was doing, I'd still be living in Atlanta today. How did I think I was going to move to another country where I basically only knew a bunch of twenty-somethings and establish a school with the expectation of changing a whole nation? Sometimes I still shake my head like, what was I thinking?

Several years after I started Bethel Atlanta Cameroon, I told a new friend my story and he asked several questions. "Have you ever started a school before? Did you study education or curriculum planning? Had you even been to Africa before? Did you have any grant funding or institutional support? Did you know much about the culture? Was it safe?"

As he fired question after question, and every answer was a sheepish "no," I realized how crazy and "foolish" what I had done was. I honestly believe that God suspended my analytical, obsessive-compulsive planner, intellectual nature for me to take this leap of faith. It was child-like faith that allowed me to do everything I did during that time.

I was completing the 2nd year of BASSM and my class project was actually planning the school launch. I had the help of my fellow students to get things started.

And then there was the matter of shipping my furniture. I did some research and it was going to be expensive! One day I was chatting with Mimi and asked, *What can I do about sending my furniture? It seems impossible. Maybe I should just give up and get stuff made there.* I grimaced at the thought of sleeping on a foam mattress or sitting on a hard wooden couch.

The phone rang from an unknown number, so I paused our chat – strangely enough. I hate talking on the phone and rarely answer numbers I don't recognize. When I answered the call, a man with a Cameroonian accent introduced himself as Ernest Ehabe. He apologized that it had taken him so long to call. His sister was my father's home health nurse and had given him my number back in November (this was April) but he had never gotten a chance to call. We chatted for a few minutes and then I told him of my plans to move to Cameroon for ministry.

He was overjoyed and excited to have a fellow minister of the gospel moving to his country. "Is there anything I can do to help you? Anything?"

I didn't know this man and wasn't sure what he could help me with. I was about to say no, when I felt a nudge from the Holy Spirit. Instead I said, "Well, since you asked, I'm looking for a shipping company to move my things to Cameroon. Do you have any experience with that?"

He chuckled. "As a matter of fact, I just started my own shipping company to transport things for ministry from the US to Cameroon. I'd be happy to ship your things."

My mouth fell open. Welcome to the God Zone. Crazy, ridiculous, perfectly-timed miracles like that have become my life!

Not only did he offer to ship my stuff, when the time came, he helped get a U-Haul truck and came and personally helped me load much of my four-bedroom house onto the truck and then onto the shipping container. I'll share the rest of the miracle when I get to it.

One day when I logged on to chat, Mimi was excitedly waiting for me. "I found a house." She described it as a three-bedroom house with a huge parlor, right off the main road. I asked what that meant. "You walk out of the house, onto the sidewalk and there's the road. It's almost impossible to find houses on the main road. And especially for this price. This is a miracle."

No rocky, muddy/dusty, twisty, uphill path with a place I had to put my hand on the ground, risking all sorts of goat and chicken poop contamination? No face offs with huge pigs? I smiled. God had dealt with yet another one of my concerns that I hadn't even voiced.

We didn't have a place for the school yet, but I had a home with a big parlor. Worse come to worse, we'd have school in my parlor until we found a building. My faith was building. I was about to leave everything I knew and loved for a whole different life in a place that felt like a whole different world. Except for the occasional snatches of panic and anxiety, I was excited, happy, and had a general sense of peace.

Most of the panic and anxiety moments were about finances. I had grown up as a doctor's daughter, had scholarships that covered my living expenses through college and medical school and then I was a doctor. I'd been well provided for since leaving home at age seventeen. Now, I had quit my job and direct deposit was no more.

I had paid off everything but my mortgage and had two years of savings. I was ready to invest it all in the dream I was building. That was during the mortgage crisis in the US, so there was no way I could sell my house. God sent me a renter – another author from my writing group, so I didn't have to worry about that any more.

But how was I going to build this ministry? How was I going to keep it going after the savings ran out? I was going from medical doctor with a six-figure salary to missionary living on donations. That left me with an uneasy feeling.

Let me stop for a second and explain my heart. Whenever I teach on purpose and destiny, people get fired up and ready to go for it. I always have that moment of "balance" where I say, "Please don't go quit your job tomorrow. Have a plan. Pay off your debts. Save some money."

I get concerned sometimes when people want to live "by faith." I believe there's a certain wisdom that accompanies faith that keeps us from being homeless and hungry. I've heard stories of people taking that leap of faith and flying off into their God adventure with no money in their pockets. God provides for them miraculously and they have the most amazing faith stories to tell. I admire those people greatly and have great faith stories of my own where God brought abundance out of nothing.

I believe the key is intimacy with God.

I tell my kids at BASSM-Cameroon, if I ask any question and you answer, "Intimacy," nine times out of ten, you're going to be right. Living "by faith" has to come from intimate conversations with Father God. If He says, "Quit your job right now," then it's because He fully intends to take care of you. He may instead tell you, "Work for two more years, pay off everything and save this amount to live on."

People think I'm crazy for investing my retirement money into Bethel Atlanta Cameroon, but from my intimate conversations with the Father, I believed that was what I was supposed to do. I've had freak out moments about my retirement since that initial conversation and every time, He insists, more strongly each time, "*I am your retirement*."

Whatever you do in the name of "faith," do from a place of intimacy. Don't make a decision and jump into it without hearing from God. Hear what He says and obey. In that, you'll have the security of knowing He's fully responsible and will take care of your every need.

I don't want any emails from anybody telling me they read my book and quit their job and now they're broke, living in their car, and taking showers at the local gas station. When you're taking that leap of faith to jump into purpose and destiny, have some serious conversations with God. Make every financial and life decision from a place of intimacy – not from "blind faith" or a compulsion that will lead your life into difficulty.

If I'm harping on this too much, it's because it's important. God will provide for the vision He's given you. But walk in wisdom from INTIMACY when you're making big decisions that can affect your finances and overall well-being. I've seen God give so much grace when I've made a rash decision. Even if I "mess up," His grace covers me and He still provides. I'd rather live in wisdom from intimacy than covering grace, though.

So after I spent a little unnecessary time panicking about finances, I had a conversation with God.

"Father, I appreciate how You've always taken care of me. Always. I have no reason to fear because You've always been good. But I'm nervous. I've always had a sure way that You would provide for me. You're asking me to live 'by faith.' You know that's scary. For me to do this, I need a deeper revelation of You as Jehovah Jireh. I need You to become my direct deposit. You've always been Jehovah Jireh, but this is a whole different world for me. Help me to trust You. And take good care of me..."

And then He gave me peace. What a gift. No direct answer, but just a peace that He had heard and He was there. Since I made this leap of faith, I've come to truly understand the Scripture about the peace that surpasses understanding (Phil. 4:6-7).

God gave me surges of strength, faith, and courage during those times. I could feel His calm peace washing over me. He filled my heart with anticipation and excitement while letting me know that even though the place I was going would be difficult, He would be with me.

After I packed everything up for the ship, I moved into my parents' house and counted down the days until it was time to leave for Cameroon.

Ten

I couldn't sleep the entire thirty hours of my trip when I was actually moving to LIVE in Cameroon. By the time I arrived, I was jittery with excitement and lack of sleep. Mimi was excited to show me the house she had picked out for me. It was indeed right off the main road and it was huge.

But I didn't realize how much of a diva I was until she gave me the tour. First of all, the color pattern was all wrong. The walls were a stark white with a wide band of gray trim at the top and bottom. It would clash miserably with my earth-toned furniture. How could I put browns and reds in a white and gray room? For those of you that think you can't ever be a missionary because you like nice things too much, nobody could be more of a diva than me.

Mimi couldn't understand my need for all this color blending nonsense. What difference did the colors make? The bedroom colors were all wrong, too and the bathrooms were yucky. God, what had I done? I tried to keep a smile plastered on my face because Mimi was so excited that she had found such a great house. And it was a great house. Still is. It just wasn't what I expected.

She appeared confused when I asked whether we could get permission to paint the walls. The house had just been painted. I felt awful for being so spoiled and picky. But there was no way I could handle my furniture clashing with the colors in the parlor. And then she had someone make these rich, golden yellow curtains. They would match my furniture, but looking at them against the gray and white made my head ache.

I kept smiling at Mimi, but whispered a prayer in my heart. *God, I'm so sorry. This is a great house and all I can do is complain. Sorry. I really want to be a laid down lover. I want this not to matter. But it does! It matters. You know my home is my sanctuary. I need it to be warm and inviting and comfortable and beautiful. Help me not to care.*

I felt His peace wash over me. I knew He'd come up with some solution like painting it or something, so I decided not to worry anymore. I shook off the disappointment and got excited. I was in Cameroon! My dreams were coming true! I was about to be launched into the most amazing purpose and destiny! I was going to fulfill all my prophetic words!

I took a warm bucket bath and changed into my pajamas. It had been a long trip and I was tired. I wondered if I'd still be too excited to sleep since it was my first night sleeping in Cameroon in MY home. My furniture was still on the ship somewhere in the Atlantic Ocean. We borrowed a couple of foam mattresses and laid them on the floor and covered ourselves with blankets. It was rainy season, so somewhat chilly.

I lay down on the foam mattress and sank down to the cold floor. I looked up at the ceiling and saw a wall gecko running overhead. On a mission trip to Honduras, my pastor and friend, Tracy Cooper, had a wall gecko fall from the ceiling right down on her head. I pulled the covers over me and left only a small hole for my nose for breathing. Soon after, I heard a mosquito singing in my ear. I thought about life-threatening malaria and covered my entire head with the sheet, trusting I'd get enough oxygen through the cotton.

And yet, in that moment, with only a squished foam mattress between me and the cold floor, a wall gecko skittering overhead, and a mosquito singing in my ear, I felt more joy, more satisfaction, more excitement than I had ever felt in my life. I was dancing into my destiny.

The next few days were filled with activity and preparations for the school and also me getting used to my new town. We walked up and down that main road of the city, looking for a building for the school. I noticed a very large, empty, fenced house, five buildings down from my house. I asked Mimi about it and she said it had been empty for a while and was being renovated. Long story short, she got the owner's number and next thing I know, we were looking at it for a potential school building.

When I first walked in, my mouth fell open. It had a large parlor and dining area with a fireplace. The walls were a light, golden yellow. The master bedroom was huge with a bathtub. There were three other big bedrooms, each with their own bathroom. The kitchen was large with a large pantry. There were beautiful arches in the doorways and beautiful light fixtures. The big fenced-in backyard had a perfect view of Mount Cameroon.

I told Mimi. "I want it. I want this to be my house and we'll use the other house for the school."

She negotiated the price and we moved in a few days later. The color was perfect for my earth-toned furniture and even the curtains Mimi had bought matched perfectly. I had a hot water heater installed in the master bedroom that extended to all the showers in the house.

Was that necessary for my life as a missionary? Some would think me ridiculous for being that picky. Who cares about the paint colors on the walls? I'm here to "suffer for Jesus."

But the truth was, it mattered to me, so it mattered to God. He knows my unique personality. He knows I'm an artist and a very visual person. He knows my need for sanctuary and balanced colors and natural light. He knows that I'll work long and hard for Him and then be refreshed and revived by my earth tones and pillow-top mattress. He knows a hot shower every morning rather than a warm bucket bath will give me longevity in this new, strange, foreign home far, far away from everything I was familiar and comfortable with.

He made sure I had it. I had two, big beautiful houses on the main road, five doors away from each other. The first house was perfect for a school building and the new house was perfect for his diva daughter.

And so, the diva missionary was born. Twenty years after I got that first prophetic word. That was one of the greatest lessons for me. The prophetic word was given, I believed and received it, but it took twenty years before I set foot on African soil. Why?

It was all about preparation. God had to build things in me. Knowledge of His nature. Knowledge of the Kingdom. The ability to endure hardness like a good soldier, with a heart full of praise and worship. I had learned how to love people well, even if they were different from me.

Life had taught me how to trust God when everything is falling apart. I didn't go much into the details of my marriage and divorce, but that was a huge learning period for me. Almost having to file bankruptcy and having my heart ripped in a million pieces by my husband's betrayal, and then the uphill journey of putting my heart and my life back together again made me resilient and strong, able to overcome during the worst emotional nightmare. Suffice it to say that MANY lessons were learned during that season.

It was important for me to gain everything I'd learned at Bethel Atlanta – the freedom, the extravagant worship, prophesying from love and not from judgment, identity, family and community, and the message of the Father heart of God.

Sometimes we judge God unfaithful when His promises aren't fulfilled in the time we expect them to be. But I've learned that God is the master Author. When I'm writing a novel, I spend a lot of time getting to know my characters. I map out a detailed timeline of their lives. I decide what's supposed to happen in the story, and then I go back through their whole fictional life and decide what had to happen when for them to get to the point where they are in the story. It takes a long time, staring at the timeline, adding up years, deciding what events happen when, and orchestrating the character's life story.

God is the greatest Orchestrator and has a detailed timeline of each of our lives. He knows exactly how and exactly when things in our lives should happen. If it seems like things are delayed, trust that He's a good, good Father and that He knows exactly what He's doing. His time is perfect and the best for you. This is from a person who had almost given up trusting and believing that the things He had promised in twenty years of prophetic words would ever happen.

The ship finally arrived. When we were in Atlanta, Mr. Ehabe had asked for a deposit to put the things on the ship and then I was to pay the rest when everything cleared customs. By that time, I had done some serious research and realized that I probably owed him $6-8,000.

I had kicked myself a million times for shipping all that stuff. That would be a chunk of the savings I planned to live on while the school was getting established. I was upset that my spoiled, diva ways had caused me to ship everything and run up such a bill. Two couches, a loveseat and two armchairs, several beds, a washer and dryer (so I wouldn't have to wash and wring clothes by hand) a huge, stainless steel refrigerator, boxes of books (those I couldn't do without) sheets, towels, comforters, pictures – everything I needed to feel like home.

I was ashamed that I thought I needed them and now I was going to have less money for the work of the ministry. Me and Mimi rented a truck and went to pick up all the stuff. As we loaded it from the container to the truck, piece by piece, my heart dropped further and further into my stomach. What I had shipped was even more than I remembered. This was gonna cost a grip.

After we loaded everything and got ready to leave, I walked up to Mr. Ehabe, biting my lip. We made small talk for a while and then I finally got to the question I didn't want the answer to.

"Ummmmm, what's the balance I owe you for everything?"

He laughed and clapped me on the back. "My dear Missionary Sherri. You don't owe me anything.

I'm so grateful for you moving here to serve my country."

What?

He walked away, giving instructions to the men who were offloading the container. I stood there with my mouth open. Did he just say I didn't owe him anything? Did he just wipe away an $8,000 debt with the wave of his hand?

I felt God, Jesus, and the Holy Spirit laughing at me. I honestly think they get a kick out of it when I'm obsessively afraid of something and They miraculously fix it in a way I NEVER see coming.

It's like they're sitting up there elbowing each other like, ***"Look at her. She's shaking. She's really scared, isn't she? Poor baby. She doesn't trust Us yet. But she will. Watch this."***

And then they sit, excitedly waiting for the miraculous moment to happen. That moment when I'm left standing speechless, mouth agape, completely dazed, overwhelmed and unable to process the latest miracle. I think it makes them laugh until their sides ache.

With yet another miracle under my belt and a lot more confidence in my heart, I got settled into my house and set up everything to start the school. It was time to get to work to establish Bethel Atlanta School of Supernatural Ministry – Cameroon.

Eleven

The first thing we had to do was recruit students. I had assumed that most of Youth Aglow would attend the school, but after hanging out with them for a while, I realized people had lives and plans and responsibilities. We had to find a way to let people know Bethel Atlanta Cameroon was there, what it was, and how it would change their lives.

Mr. Ehabe took it upon himself to organize two programs, introducing me and Bethel Atlanta Cameroon to the community. We held a seminar at the University of Buea and invited students and members of the community. He also held a dinner program to introduce me to the pastors and spiritual leaders in Buea.

Every time I think about him planning, organizing and financing my introduction, I send up a prayer of thanks and release heavenly blessings on him! There was no reason under heaven for him to do that, other than his love for God and his country. He asked for nothing in return and had no hidden agendas for helping me.

Most of our students from the first year were recruited from Youth Aglow and from the program held at University of Buea. We started the first year with forty-five students. I was excited!

The first year was busy for me. I did most of the teaching, aided by some of the DVD's from the BSSM curriculum. I helped lead worship, led intercession, did counseling and sozo (inner healing), and gave oversight to administration. Just thinking about all the work that first year makes me tired.

But I was sowing and planting and building something. I was finally living my dreams and fulfilling my prophecies. The excitement fueled me every day. I had no idea whether it would work or grow or be sustainable, but I put my whole life into it because I believed what God said it would be.

I put everything I had into it financially as well – my savings and retirement. I made a complete commitment to the promises of God for my life, Cameroon, and the continent of Africa. Again, that's one of those things I often get strange looks about, if I dare to tell someone. They either say, or give me a look that says, "Why would you sink your retirement and savings into something not guaranteed to last without keeping anything for yourself?"

My only answer is that I'm crazy in love with Him and His love makes me do crazy things. I trust that He's got my retirement in His hands. As I'll tell later, He's worked so many miracles of provision that I fully believe Him. And not only for what I need. He cares about my personal desires as well.

The first year was amazing. The most beautiful thing about it was watching the lives of my students transformed, right before my very eyes. There's no high in the world like it. We taught about the baptism of the Holy Spirit and people received the explosive infilling for the first time. It was exciting to be able to facilitate people getting one of the greatest gifts God has given us.

When I taught on the Father heart, I saw people breaking under the weight of His love. When they realized it's not about rules and regulations, but that He truly loves us and wants to be in relationship with us, I saw hearts change.

Cameroon and many African countries tend to have a VERY legalistic take on Christianity. People told me about how they wrote down their sins every day so they could make sure they repented well and stayed in right relationship with God. Others talked about their fear of God, not reverence, but stark fear of not serving Him correctly and always being at risk of losing their salvation. I had a conversation with one young man who asked me to pray for him because he couldn't access the anointing God had for him because he was unable to complete the 50-day, dry fast God had called him to. Because he couldn't manage the whole fifty days without food, he couldn't be as anointed as he was supposed to be.

I could write pages and pages of stories of Christians completely in love with God, and desiring to serve Him, but living lives full of fear, guilt, shame, and trying to live up to an impossible standard to please a very, scary God.

Imagine the transformation when my students were taught they were already beloved sons and daughters in whom God is well pleased – just because they're His and not because of anything they do.

I met MUCH resistance when teaching the message of grace. Many Cameroonian Christians are very well versed in the Scriptures and we actually had arguments, them quoting the Old Testament and me quoting New Testament Scriptures about grace and forgiveness.

Some accepted this new revelation of grace and the Father's love and goodness with joy. Some argued, but stayed, and others left. It's been amazing to see a few that left eventually receive the message of grace elsewhere and come back to discuss with me their newfound revelation. I guess God intended for them to get the understanding somehow and He kept chasing them until they accepted it.

My most favorite moments are releasing students in the prophetic. I love teaching on the prophetic – to demystify it and help people realize it's simply having a conversation with a Father that loves them. When I see the excitement in a student's eyes after they give an accurate prophetic word – how shocked they are that they actually heard GOD – my heart is full. That never gets old, year after year, person after person, connecting them to the heart of their Father and tuning their ears to His voice. I could and will spend the rest of my life doing that.

Releasing the students into power evangelism is also exciting. When they give a prophetic word to a stranger on the street and the person asks, with tears and wonder in their eyes, "How did you know that?" the student's life is transformed. Having students come back from hospital outreach after seeing their first miracle is overwhelming. Giving away keys to the Kingdom is one of the greatest privileges I'll ever enjoy.

In the last quarter, we do a track on purpose and destiny. This proved to be harder than I thought. I realized that in the Cameroonian education system, people aren't taught to be creative, imaginative, or to take initiative. The poverty of the society doesn't teach or allow people to dream. Young Cameroonians are taught that to be successful, you either take a government job and learn to be corrupt to get extra money, or you travel to Canada, the UK, or the US for more opportunities and a better life.

So when this American missionary came along, asking them to dream about their future, they didn't know what to do. I was asking them to discover the dream of their hearts and to press into God to find their purpose and destiny. They said it was stressful and difficult for them. I have a list of questions that help lead a person on a journey into their heart to discover who they are and what they were born to do. Many of the students couldn't understand the questions or couldn't answer them. That type of thinking was foreign to them. They got visibly frustrated and upset and many never finished the exercise.

But it was amazing to watch those that did. I love to tell the success stories of BASSM-C grads from all the years. Please, endure this proud Mama for a moment.

Winnie Khamal delved into the questions voraciously, developed a vision journal with pictures clipped from magazines and her own drawings. A few years later, she ended up opening a fashion house whose décor and fashion rivaled a boutique like one you'd find in New York City.

Bessie Nchenge, who served as an intern in the first year, fell in love with inner healing. My mom, in her many visits to Cameroon, trained her in sozo and counseling. Bessie devoured books, videos, and any online teaching she could find on inner healing. She took the training she got to a whole new level.

She's now one of the most skilled and gifted inner healers I've ever met and has amazing dreams for bringing inner healing to all of Africa. She's raised up an amazing Transformation Center at BASSM-C and she and her team have traveled to Nigeria several times to partner with a sister ministry, Lapis Lazuli, to bring inner healing to that country. Bessie has recently been named the regional sub-director for Bethel Sozo for Cameroon by the Director of Bethel Sozo Africa.

Kingsley Ndive had just made a serious commitment to Christ. When I first met him at Youth Aglow, he bragged that he could play any instrument and loved to sing. He has become one of the most gifted worship leaders you ever want to see. He has the ability to bring down heaven in EVERY worship session. It's a running joke among the staff that on class nights, after an hour of worship, someone has to go take the mic from him, otherwise worship will last until it's time for school to end. Sometimes we don't stop him and we just bask in fiery praise and extravagant worship for the whole three hours. Kingsley has also become a gifted teacher and manager and is truly a gift to my staff.

During her year at BASSM-C, Quinta discovered that she was called to train children and to launch them into their destiny. She's now a primary school teacher in a nearby town. Another Quinta developed a successful gourmet cake designing and decorating business. My heart smiles every time I see her creative, out-of-the-box designs on Facebook.

Others are successful doctors, lawyers, entrepreneurs, corporate managers, government translators, housewives and Kingdom mothers. I'm proud to say we have graduates invading all 7 spheres of influence in society.

One of the highlights of the first year was a team of ten missionaries coming over from BASSM. It was beautiful to see BASSM students from Atlanta bond with those from Cameroon the way they did. We had great meals together, laughing at the Americans eating Cameroonian pepper and turning bright red with tears running down their faces. We went on amazing treasure hunts, prayer walks, and hospital visits resulting in miraculous testimonies.

My favorite part was the beach trip, where we splashed and swam, the boys played football (soccer) and then we all sat down at huge tables to eat roasted fish with pepper sauce with our bare hands, sealing the bond of family between us. We've continued to have teams from BASSM each year since and it's one of the biggest highlights for students from both schools.

We also took a missions trip to Mbengwi, a small village in the Northwest region of Cameroon. Me, my three interns and a group of students did evangelism, helped minister at a crusade, and me and Bessie were the doctor and nurse at a health outreach (did I mention that I snatched her from her nursing job to come work at BASSM?). My mom was in Cameroon visiting and went on that trip with us and served as a counselor with a few of the other students. The best part of the trip was the bonding – the epic waterfall climb, the outreach trips to people's homes where they encouraged each other to be courageous and pray for a family of blind children, the meals together and early morning prayer.

The graduation for the first class of BASSM-C was one of the greatest days of my life. My mom had already visited us two times that year and was there for graduation. I stood at the front, dressed in a flowing African gown, as my mom presented to me the graduating class of the 2010-11 school year – forty students in all. I stood at the front with tears streaming down my face as they marched in, looking like African princes and princesses. I still get emotional thinking about that moment and every graduation after it.

The whole day was surreal. I had launched and successfully graduated students from a School of Supernatural Ministry in Africa. I thought back to all my prophetic words that I thought would never come to pass. As I gave the graduation speech, choking back tears of joy, I was standing right in the middle of my purpose and destiny!

At the end of graduation, I gave a charge:

Heal the sick. Raise the dead. Cause the blind to see, the deaf to hear and the lame to walk. Cast out demons and bring the Kingdom wherever you go! BE a walking, living encounter with Jesus every day of your life because you might be the only Jesus a person may ever see.

It was an exciting day filled with joy and celebration. Unfortunately, the enemy was about to strike me at the knees in a vicious attempt to end BASSM-C before it went any further.

Twelve

The day after graduation, me, Mimi and my mom drove to Douala because I had a ministry engagement. Afterwards, we went to eat dinner at an Indian restaurant. I love Cameroonian food, but was glad for something different.

We got a call about one of my spiritual daughters. She worked diligently and loyally at my house, keeping it spotless and keeping me and my roommates full of the finest Cameroonian cuisine. She was a faithful intercessor at Youth Aglow and flowed in the prophetic. She had been sick for several weeks and had actually moved into my home for us to take care of her and monitor her closely. Her illness eventually progressed to the point where she was hospitalized. We planned to go straight to the hospital to see her when we returned from Douala.

When Mimi hung up the phone, her face was filled with shock. "Ernestine's dead."

My heart stopped and time stood still.

An angel must have protected us as we drove straight through Douala's life-threatening traffic to the morgue at the Buea General Hospital. On the way home, I summoned my faith to pray for a resurrection, but the Holy Spirit flashed me a picture of Ernestine, smiling bright as the sun in Jesus' arms. He said to leave her be. She'd endured a very difficult life and I had never seen that joyous of a smile on her face.

When we walked into the morgue and they uncovered her for me to see, she actually had a smile plastered on her face. I told my sons who had gathered there to pray for her resurrection to stop. She was in glory and we were to leave her there.

I can't describe the emotions that the director of a school of supernatural ministry goes through the day after her first graduation, after charging her students to heal the sick and raise the dead, to experience a death that close to home. We had been praying for Ernestine for weeks, declaring life and cursing death.

Her death felt like a slap in the face. I felt like a failure. I had given up everything to move to Africa to teach the supernatural and satan had struck back, making me believe that my sacrifice was in vain.

It was also personally difficult because she was close to me. We had many talks while she was in the kitchen cooking and I had gotten to know her heart. While she was sick, me, Mimi, and mom took care of her. I held her at the sink while she was vomiting violently, praying and comforting her. I coaxed her into eating and drinking when she had no appetite and said she wanted to die. One night, she woke up from a nightmare, screaming that she was dying. I climbed into bed with her and held her and rocked her, praying and singing and prophesying life to her, until she fell asleep in my arms.

She was mine – a part of my heart – and the enemy had stolen her right out of my arms. That affected me beyond words.

Over the next year, my heart was struck again as a close ministry relationship fell terribly apart. Again, honor won't allow me to go into the details. Much was said about me and two of my top leaders, to the point where some registered students decided not to come to the school the following year. Graduates who heard some of the fallout were distrusting and not sure they wanted to serve as interns as planned.

The summer after the second year, I was tired, frustrated and hurt by everything that had happened. I was ready to shut down the school. When I was leaving to go back for the beginning of the third year, I told my bestie, Yvette, I was going to pack up my stuff and I'd be back by her birthday in October.

I felt like a complete failure. I knew I was quitting to come back home, but I didn't know what I would do. Going back to medicine would send me into an even deeper depression. I hadn't written any new books and that wasn't enough to live on anyway. I visualized becoming a barista at Starbucks and living in my parents' basement for the next few years.

And then I had a God encounter…

I was soaking and worshipping, trying to get direction and pull myself up out of the slump. I was taken up to heaven and stood outside a door with loud music and celebration going on inside of it. The doors swung open and there was a host of angels in a huge, decorated hall celebrating. When they saw me standing outside, they cheered. One grabbed me and ushered me inside. I looked down at myself, knowing I was unfit to attend an angelic party.

I was wearing a military uniform that was dirty, bloody and tattered. The angels quickly stripped off the uniform, fixed my wounds, washed and dressed me. When they finished, I looked like a warrior princess, like the queen in the movie, *The 300*. They topped it off with a golden crown and a laurel wreath to go around my neck. Then they began cheering and celebrating me.

I was completely confused. I walked out onto a balcony and saw the Father standing there. He had the kindest, gentlest eyes and a broad smile on His face.

"Why are you out here? You should be inside enjoying your celebration."

"I don't understand why they're celebrating me. I'm a failure. Ernestine died on my watch. This relationship fell apart and there was nothing I could do to fix it. Half the BASSM-C community thinks I'm a horrible, abusive leader. Students are dropping out and there are rumors about me, Bessie, and Sue everywhere. My girls are hurting because of me. I don't want to do this anymore. But what else can I do? I don't want to be a doctor anymore. Where will I end up? Being a barista at Starbucks? Selling tickets at the movies? I don't even know what to do with my life now. I'm a failure."

The Father threw His head back and laughed. *"Failure? Are you serious? You're one of heaven's greatest successes. Those angels out there love to watch you. They love to watch you love and pour into people and they admire you. This party is to celebrate the great exploits you've accomplished in Cameroon."*

I stood there with a look of complete confusion on my face.

I'll never forget the love in His eyes as the Father put a hand on my cheek and said with serious firmness, *"Babygirl, you MUST learn how to see things as heaven sees them. Leave behind the earthly idea of success and learn what true success is. In heaven. Here, we don't view things as you do. In heaven, you are greatly respected and hugely successful. CHANGE YOUR PERSPECTIVE."*

Those have become words I live by. I always try to view things from heaven's perspective rather than earth's. When I get frustrated, worried, or fearful, it's usually a failure in the area of perspective.

He patted me on the back. *"Get back in there and enjoy your party."*

I smiled big. "Okay, yeah. Are You coming?"

He smiled that broad smile again. *"I'm God. I'm already there."*

I laughed and swung open the huge, golden door to go back inside the grand hall. What a party it was. The angels picked me up threw me up in the air, cheering my name loudly. There was a large fountain of glory juice flowing near the buffet table. Me and an angel turned our heads upside down under the fountain and guzzled glory juice until we almost choked. We laughed until we cried with joy. We danced and sang and shouted until joy completely saturated my whole being.

I can't remember how long I stayed in that vision, but after I came out, it was settled in my heart. I wasn't a failure. Death of a spiritual daughter and a relationship split didn't disqualify me from ministry.

I surrendered my life and gave God a fresh yes. No matter what was ahead of me, I was staying in Cameroon.

God gave me great grace when I returned. We had a big dinner in our brand new hall and gathered members of our community that had been affected by the whole split. I told them I wanted to walk in honor so I couldn't explain the whole situation, but I did address some of their concerns. I also allowed them to ask questions.

From their questions, I was shocked and hurt at some of the things they had believed about me, but I truthfully explained as much as I could. We all prayed together at the end of that meeting and I felt love and healing flowing in the room.

We did have our fewest number of students that year, but it was also one of our best and sweetest years. Some of the graduates of that class are now staff members and others are still an intricate part of the BASSM-C community.

We were in a brand new building because the previous owners wanted their house back so they could build a daycare. This building was larger with more office space for pretty much the same price. It was also in a quieter neighborhood. Even though it's nice to be on the main street to avoid walking on mud and stones, the noise levels were too high for a ministry school where we sometimes soak and need complete quiet.

That was an explosive praise year. We had many dancers in that class who were expressive and passionate. We danced until we sweat and then fell on our faces caught up in sweet worship. That year, our praise and worship went to whole new levels, invoking the presence of God to the point where we experienced more glory than I had ever experienced anywhere in my whole life.

The sweet end to the year was graduation, although I must say it started off as a major catastrophe. We'd paid the money for the hall we had used for graduation the first two years, but when we went there on the Friday night before graduation

Saturday, it was filled with papers, stacked five to seven feet high. The testing board for the country's Anglophone educational system used the same hall to store and prepare their standardized tests. We were told they'd be out by morning and that we'd be able to clean, rehearse, and decorate. I panicked a little, but trusted that God would work everything out.

We arrived early the next morning to find that not even one paper had been moved. The men who were supposed to be moving the papers jeered at us and told us nothing would be out by graduation.

Graduation was supposed to start at 1 pm, but we had no venue. I wish I could say I was calm, but I wasn't. I was angry and upset and yelled at the workers at the hall we had paid for, probably more than I should have. My kids know I'm trusting God for deliverance from anger issues, so they sent me home and said they would take care of everything.

About an hour later, they called me to come see the new hall they had found. It was down the street from the first hall and was twice as big. It had high ceilings, was big and airy and already had tables so we wouldn't have to rent any, but boy was it filthy!

We called the graduating class and any alumni that would help and everyone showed up on the morning of their graduation to clean. One thing I love about Africans is their sense of loyalty and community and the fact that they sing, joke, and laugh while they work. My stress was lost in their harmonies and laughter and it became a beautiful family experience.

Within a few hours, the hall was clean, rented chairs were set up and decorations were in place. The venue looked fabulous!

By the time the graduating class and all their guests showed up, the hall was packed. We would have never fit that old venue. God, of course, knew that ahead of time and had already worked things out for us. One of these days, I'm going to learn to stop panicking and fretting and trust that He's always looking out for me. No matter the crisis.

After everything that had happened, Year 3 was one of the sweetest years. Bethel Atlanta Cameroon was going better than I could have expected. But I was growing restless, as I've learned visionaries do. My heart was starting to ache for even more.

Thirteen

Near the end of 2012, I started to feel itchy. Like I was supposed to go somewhere or do something different. For no particular reason. Things were going well at Bethel Cameroon. I was in a good place. But something was stirring in the Spirit.

I came home on holiday and preached at Bethel Atlanta one Sunday. The assistant pastor posted a picture of me speaking on his Facebook page. When I "liked" it, I noticed a comment from someone named Rosie Awori.

It read, *Oh I love her! Is the podcast out yet?*

I commented back. *Hey! Thanks for the love! The podcast isn't out yet, but I'll let you know when it is. Your name isn't Cameroonian. Where are you from?*

She answered, *Kenya!*

I added her and private messaged her. We went back and forth for a while. She was enrolled in the Kingdom Academy, a school of ministry in Nairobi, and had been instructed to look for messages by Shawn Bolz. In Googling him, she was led to Bethel Atlanta's podcast. She listened to his message and several others and had stumbled across some of mine. She had listened and loved them.

We chatted back and forth for a while and soon, I started feeling that same feeling I had when I first started chatting with Mimi. All of a sudden, I wanted to go to Kenya. I wasn't sure why, but I knew I needed to go.

We chatted regularly and the draw to go to Kenya grew stronger. I talked to my then ministry partner and we decided that even though it made no sense, we were going. I got my first editing job, a referral from my writing partner and before I knew it, I had enough money for a trip.

I remembered I had met a Kenyan pastor when I went to the Leader's Advance at Bethel Church in Redding prior to launching Bethel Atlanta Cameroon. He was the director of a large orphanage and some friends from Bethel Atlanta had visited there when they were students at BSSM. I felt like we were supposed to visit that orphanage.

I dug out Daddy Weston Gitonga's number and called. I explained who I was and asked if we could come visit. I realized I probably sounded crazy, a pretty much stranger, calling out of the blue, asking to come from a different country just to visit. He said that wonderful African phrase, "You are welcome," and my heart jumped. I didn't know why, but there was purpose in our going.

There was also a fellow Bethel Atlanta missionary in Kenya, near Mombasa. She had graduated from the Harvest School at Iris Ministries in Mozambique and was there rescuing sex slaves. I reached out to Brittanie Richardson and made plans to go visit her as well.

My ministry partner had been to Kenya a few years before and had gotten donations of audio Bibles in Swahili for a Maasai village she had visited. We made plans to go to the village. She wanted to spend the night, but I told her I wasn't sure the diva missionary was up for a night in an extremely rural village.

As we were making arrangements, the whole thing seemed strange. Why were we even going? Why were we spending money we needed for our ministries in Cameroon? What did Kenya have to do with anything? But I felt the wind of the Holy Spirit on it, so I decided to follow.

Rosie's mom offered to let us stay at their house for the first few days and then we were to move into a hostel not too far from them. I was nervous about the accommodations. You never know where you're going to end up when someone offers to let you stay at their house. The price of the youth hostel had me worried about mice and roaches and uncomfortable mattresses. My ministry partner was a "true missionary" – not of the diva persuasion like me. I knew she'd be able to deal with whatever. Me? Not so much. But I knew the Holy Spirit was in charge of the whole thing, so I decided to quit worrying and just trust.

When we arrived at Rosie's house in Nairobi, I couldn't believe the goodness of God. It was a big, beautiful house with a beautiful garden, beautiful hand-made furniture and classy décor. The diva missionary was right at home! We had a wonderful dinner with Rosie, her mom, and her little sister and I felt like we were at home with family. We stayed up talking with Rosie half the night, as if we had been friends for years. As she was leaving to go to bed, she stuck her head back through the door and said, " Oh by the way, my mom said to tell you that you guys are welcome to stay with us for your whole trip to Kenya."

Our mouths fell open. God, through Mama Mercy, had saved us hundreds of dollars and we'd be staying in a beautiful house with a lovely, Kingdom family.

Welcome to the God Zone...

When Rosie took us out the first day, I was shocked. This was a different Africa. It was clean and beautifully landscaped and there were high-rises and skyscrapers. We went to a mall with international restaurants and coffee shops. I got a decaf, soy latte (my favorite coffee) at Java House! Was this Africa? It felt more like Atlanta. It was developed with good electricity, running water and fast Internet – at least in the part of Nairobi where we were living. The city was metropolitan with great shopping, dining and all the modern comforts I had grown up enjoying. But it was Africa. Proudly African. I was intrigued and fell in love with Kenya from that first day.

I'm sure the Africans reading this are rolling their eyes and feeling a bit offended. Excuse my ignorance, but don't all Americans think Africa is a bushy jungle with mud huts and wild animals? Full of babies with swollen bellies and sad eyes, surrounded by flies and death lurking – lying on the dirt crying, while their mothers sit and watch hopelessly? God, forgive the Western media for its portrayal of Africa. I'm so blessed to know the REAL Africa – the good, the bad, the ugly. But mostly the beautiful.

Rosie took us to visit her ministry school, Kingdom Academy. I was excited as I listened to Pastor Eric Kibuga and Pastor Niyi Morayinko teaching. Their curriculum was similar to ours – the prophetic, purpose and destiny, the supernatural. I was able to meet with the leaders the next day and found kindred spirits in them. It was exciting to meet other Kingdom, prophetic, supernatural Christians in Africa. They shared their whole curriculum for the two-year school with us. God had been dealing with me about putting our curriculum into a well-written book. Holding their many curriculum books in my hand inspired me to push towards that goal.

I got to minister with Pastor Niyi one night and gave prophetic words to several of the students. The leadership team also gave me prophetic words about taking the nations of Africa. It was beautiful to form relationship with them and I felt strengthened every time I got to visit Kingdom Academy and their church, Eagle's Nest.

Our next trip was to Heroes of the Nation orphanage in Nyahururu. Daddy Weston offered to pick us up and gave us prices to rent a car and stay at their guesthouse in Nakuru. When we arrived at their beautifully appointed guesthouse in the beautiful, clean town, we talked for a while and he realized we were actually missionaries living in Cameroon, not visitors from America. Instantly, he told us we didn't have to pay to rent the car and we didn't have to pay to stay at the guesthouse. Favor in the God Zone...

I sat up talking to Daddy Weston well into the night. He told me of the BSSM he had started in Nyahururu and of the victories and challenges. He talked of his long career in ministry and about Heroes of the Nation.

As we continued to talk and drink Kenyan tea, things turned prophetic. He began to tell me I had an apostolic call on my life. He said I was called to bring change to the nations of Africa. I needed to learn French and Swahili so I could go all over Africa preaching and teaching the message of the Kingdom. The more this man of small stature with the kindest eyes and most loving smile spoke, the more my heart came alive. He was prophesying a destiny I had dreamed about. We had just met and he was telling me my whole life.

We finally said good night and I went to my room to sleep under my mosquito net, but sleep was nowhere to be found. I literally sat awake into the wee hours of the morning, my heart churning and burning with the apostolic call he had pronounced over my life. Something spiritual was happening deep inside me, and my brain was having a difficult time processing what my spirit was coming to understand.

The next day, we drove through a vast horizon of dense, green tea fields, up into the highlands of Nyahururu. The car broke down at one point and I didn't even panic. I just prayed and trusted and before long, we were on the road again.

My heart was in no way ready for what we experienced at Heroes. It sits in a tiny, picturesque village with red, clay roads and huge, overhanging trees. We drove through a colorfully painted gate into a large compound with several well-constructed buildings including classrooms, offices, dormitories, and a rectory.

Our tour guide took us into a classroom and I realized this was no orphanage. This was a boarding school of the highest caliber. The children were clean, well groomed, and neatly dressed in their school uniforms. They greeted us and asked us intelligent questions and gave articulate answers to anything we asked of them. I had never seen anything like it. We spent the evening with the girls and then went to a prayer session with all the kids.

I could write a book about our experience in this amazing "non-orphanage." The children were well-behaved, amazingly artistic and performed songs, skits, and dances for us. They were spiritual and conducted their own prayer meetings and church services. We were so fascinated that we cancelled our planned safari and spent the weekend with the kids at the non-orphanage.

Daddy Weston also took me and my ministry partner to his BSSM there. They had a small, quiet compound with classrooms and a dorm. God had been speaking to me about us having a dorm in Cameroon so we could do intensive Kingdom training. My ministry partner dreamed of building a top-notch orphanage – well actually a children's village. I dreamed of a residential kingdom training center. We both got to see our dreams in reality and left that visit inspired.

Daddy Weston asked if I wanted to come help him build other BSSM's in Kenya. I only laughed and told him I was called to Cameroon. He warned me to remember I was called to Africa and not only Cameroon, and I should let him know when I was ready to come to Kenya.

On our way back to Nairobi, we got to see a bit of the beautiful countryside of Kenya. Kenya is stunning and I wanted to tell the bus driver to stop so many times because of the picture perfect scenes passing by window. The national pride is amazing. Everything is clean, beautifully landscaped and well kept. I love how Kenyans love their country.

Our next trip was to see Brittanie in Mombasa. She actually lived in a small village outside of Mombasa, known for its sex slave trafficking. She had rescued five young girls, ages eight through fifteen and then an older girl who was twenty-two from a tragic life of sex slavery. They were living in a large, well-decorated mansion on the edge of town.

Going through town, you could feel the darkness in the atmosphere. As Brittanie told us story after story, my heart bled for what the young girls had gone through. I also wondered how she could possibly do that kind of work. We got a chance to minister to both Brittanie and the girls, but that was a difficult, heart-wrenching visit.

We did get to enjoy the beauty of Mombasa. I got to fulfill part of one of my dreams, which is to sit on beaches on all the oceans of the world. The Indian Ocean is like a huge, hot pool, with perfectly clear, blue water and pristine white sand. I was also grateful for the opportunity to bond with Brittanie more.

We came back and spent more time in Nairobi, enjoying shopping, lattes and good restaurants, and then got ready for our next adventure.

The next leg of our journey was the most life changing of all. We hired the driver who had been taking us all over Nairobi to take us to the Masaai village my ministry partner had taken an AIM missions trip to a year before. We had a Kenyan pastor as our tour guide and Rosie as our faithful companion in adventure. We drove on beautiful, winding roads through high hills overlooking plush green valleys for about two hours. We turned right off the paved road onto a dirt road and the real adventure began.

At some point, we saw a large giraffe standing in a field, chewing some leaves he had just torn from a tree. I stared at him and he stared at us. A real, live giraffe in the wild. It was crazy. We turned left onto another dirt road and things got rockier. Unfortunately, our driver's car was made for Nairobi and not for the bush. We went over a high rock and the car stopped. We got out and pushed for a while. It was hot – like painfully hot. We had already seen an ostrich, some gazelles and a giraffe. What other wild animals were lurking out there? I have this hilarious picture of me sweating under the hot sun with this crazy frown on my face. The diva missionary was NOT happy.

But then we saw a young Masaai warrior, dressed in his tribal wear, herding cows. I stared in wonder as Rosie told us that Masaai warriors are initiated into manhood by killing a lion with their bare hands. She told us a little of the history of the tribe and of some of the customs of the people.

Our driver shouted that he had gotten the car running and we got back on the road. We drove for what seemed like forever and finally pulled up outside a simple, wooden church building. My ministry partner got out and greeted her old friends. I couldn't stop staring. I felt like I had entered into the pages of an issue of *National Geographic*. Masaai garb is colorful loins of fabric, wrapped expertly around their bodies. The beaded jewelry is fit for kings and queens.

As we were greeting the villagers, a beautiful, coal black woman covered in beaded jewelry with huge, doe eyes grabbed my arm and twisted a bracelet onto my wrist. Rosie smiled and showed me that it was beaded in the pattern of the Kenyan flag. I don't know why, but I felt like this regal Masaai warrior woman had just granted me spiritual authority in her land by putting that bracelet on me.

As we prepared to go into the church, the adults lined up in a row and we lined up next to them, not sure what was about to happen. The children lined up and proceeded to walk past all the adults. Each one bowed their head in respect to the adults and the adults placed their hand on each child's head as a sign of love and covering. Honestly, I'll have to ask a Masaai if that's what those motions meant, but that's what it felt like to me. I can't explain why that simple act touched my heart so much, but it did.

We started the church service and the Masaai people began singing in their native language and started their classic, Masaai jumping and head bobbing dance. I was enthralled. I had been living in Cameroon for three years, but for some reason, maybe the dress, dance and language, I said under my breath, "Now this is Africa."

I couldn't understand a word they were saying, but I felt Jesus. We were from completely different parts of the world, with different languages and different cultures, but we served the same King. I closed my eyes and worshipped. Not for long because I didn't want to miss any of the beauty I was seeing.

I spoke briefly and my ministry partner spoke briefly and then our pastor tour guide preached a message. I whispered to God that I wanted to worship Him with different tribes and tongues all over the world. I wanted to spend the rest of my life discovering how other people groups served and worshipped Him.

After church, we went back to their village for a tour. My ministry partner gave the Swahili audio Bibles and the people were amazed when they heard the Bible in their language coming from this little black box. They gathered around a tree, listening to the Scriptures for a while. I was so excited that we had brought them the Word.

We went and toured the village and school buildings. On the way back, I walked and talked with one of the elders of the village. He had two wives because he got saved after marrying and having children with both. I asked him how he had come to know Jesus.

I'll never forget his answer. He recounted the exact date that a white missionary had come to their village. Before then, they were involved in occult worship and animism. The missionary came and preached the gospel of Jesus Christ and the whole town got saved. They spread the gospel to neighboring towns. One missionary was responsible for changing the lives of villages of people. They were no longer sacrificing animals and worshipping the mountain gods. Whole villages believed in Jesus Christ. Because of one man.

I was astonished. How did that missionary even find them? I mean, drive two hours out of Nairobi, turn right onto the dirt road, turn left at the giraffe and keep driving until you reach people?

The call on my life isn't evangelistic at all. I'm called to equip and mature believers and release them into the call on their lives. After listening to his salvation story, I knew I had to raise up as many revivalists as I could that will go to the unreached people groups of the world. Everyone deserves to hear about Jesus and to be invited into a life with Him!

In what felt like a holy moment, standing under a huge tree, breathing in the hot dry air of that small village, I made a deeper commitment to God and said a fresh "yes" to Him. This diva missionary would go wherever He asked me to go, even to the ends of the earth to extend the boundaries of His kingdom!

We went back to the main strip of the village and took a small tour of the various mud huts, which we learned were actually made of dried cow dung. We went into the elder's co-wives kitchen hut and sat and watched them make chapatti for us. We talked as much as we could – one of the wives spoke a small amount of English. The mud/dung hut was cool and much more comfortable than the sweltering heat outside. I was a little tired and still hot and leaned against the wall to rest a bit, but sat back up real fast when I remembered what the walls were made of. I know it was dried, but still...

Several women sat with us and began adorning us with beautiful, beaded jewelry. I took a picture with some of the women and a few Masaai warrior men with spears. I'll treasure that experience forever. It deepened my commitment to missions and my wanderlust and desire to explore different people and different cultures. Like, for the rest of my life...

We extended our stay in Kenya for ten days longer and finally had to return to Cameroon. I knew that Kenya would always be in my heart. I was in love and couldn't wait for an opportunity to go back.

Fourteen

When I got back from Kenya, my heart was burning to implement the things me and God had been dreaming about that I had gotten to see on that trip. God had been after me to get a curriculum book done, so me and several stuff members started working on putting it together.

The level of excellence I had experienced at the Kingdom Academy inspired me to take Bethel Atlanta Cameroon to a new level of greatness. I began more intensive leadership training with my staff and sought ways to develop new staff members to add to our team.

I had been dreaming about an intensive program where students could be housed in a dorm and could be immersed in worship, intercession, the presence, and more Kingdom teaching. After seeing the compound for Daddy Gitonga's BSSM in Nyahururu, that dream burned even stronger.

Me and my then ministry partner dreamed up a plan for a Kingdom Leadership Academy that could be held in the summer (rainy season in Cameroon) while BASSM-C wasn't in session. We discussed curriculum and how it would run. When we got to the budget though, it was very expensive. To rent a house, fully furnish it, pay staff, buy food for the students, and cover every other expense we thought of was more than we anticipated.

Most of our BASSM-C students are on full or partial scholarships and the donations from the US had to cover most of the expenses of running the school. To add another program that was quite costly didn't seem wise, so we tabled the idea.

When the Bethel Atlanta missions team came that year, there were two entrepreneurs on the team and then our precious Mama Liz, who had come the past two years, was back for her third trip. They sat down and asked me what was on my heart and how they could help.

Can I pause for a minute to say I hate asking for help? It's a serious problem I'm trusting God for deliverance from. I hate asking for money and have probably missed many blessings God wanted to bring because of it. I don't know whether it's pride or fear of vulnerability or what. Maybe it's simply going from doctor where I was the giver to being the dependent receiver. One day I'll get deliverance. I'm sure of it.

When they asked, I had to be nudged to tell them about my dreams for the Kingdom Leadership Academy (KLA). Dot Norman, Tom Guzzardo, and Mama Liz loved the idea and asked to see my budget for it. I didn't have one. When we had dreamed about it and spent a few minutes calculating how much it would cost, I got overwhelmed by the budget and didn't write anything down.

So with a team of ten missionaries visiting and a completely packed schedule of meetings, outreach, meals, a trip to the village, and a beach trip, I sat down and did a budget for KLA. Mama Dot looked at the budget and said, "Is that all? We can raise that when we get back. You'll be able to have your KLA this year. Start planning for it."

A new dream was born, just like that. Ever since then, any time God gives me a new dream, I open up Excel and make a budget for it. And then I trust. Well, I wish I could say that I do that every time. I've had some faltering in faith on our latest project. I'll explain later.

We started looking for a place to house the students, made plans to buy furniture, developed a new curriculum and planned menus all within a short period of time. Much like God had given us a miracle in giving us exactly what we were looking for in a new school building, we soon had a four-bedroom house up in the village at the bottom of the mountain where it's coolest, peaceful, with the fewest mosquitoes. It was brand new and far enough from the main road to be quiet. It also had a boy's quarters (a row of rooms across the back) for extra space.

The money came and we had furniture built and prepared the house to be lived in. We developed a curriculum to delve deeper into topics taught in first year and then also developed tracks to train students in Outreach and Community Development, Worship, Teaching and Administration, and Transformation (Inner Healing).

We decided that any participants would have to either pay or work to attend. We had learned that our scholarship students for the school weren't as dedicated and didn't work as hard as paying students. Over the years, we've gone from scholarship to work-study. Everyone has to pay or work to attend BASSM-C.

Our thirteen registrants for KLA had to work 150 hours over the course of many weeks to earn a spot in KLA. We were going to house them, feed them, and teach them for hours and we wanted them to value it.

By the time KLA was launched, we had eight dedicated souls that had completed their work hours. Seven of them moved into the house (Pastor Sako is married so he participated as a day student).

KLA was and is one of my favorite things about Bethel Atlanta Cameroon. I love the regular school year with the hall being filled with wild praisers and extravagant worshippers, but there was something beautiful and intimate about the students and staff being crowded into the parlor of our dorm/guesthouse for weekly worship and intercession and daily classes.

I can't describe the heights of glory we soared into twice a week. I've got pictures from that summer with us, kneeling, laying prostrate, and soaking on the floor. The prophetic operated at an all-time high and we loved hearing the voice of the Father corporately and individually.

The teaching times were intimate and we could see the students growing and developing right before our eyes. I think the staff grew as much as the participants and we all meshed into a closely bonded family. By the time we graduated those eight students, we were a tight knit bunch and they were stronger leaders. We ended up hiring seven of them as interns the next year and four of them are now full-time Bethel Atlanta Cameroon staff.

We had a version of KLA the following year, called The Encounter, which was even more explosive. We had Worship and Supernatural tracks and stuffed fifteen residential participants and three day-students into that house. It was more crowded, boisterous and fun with more bonding between students and staff. Our summer programs create great family. We hired four people from that second program.

KLA was held again this last summer and we were only able to hire one graduate. The staff has gotten too full. But wherever our graduates go, they'll bring the glory and excellence of the Kingdom.

In BASSM-C, the praise and worship has also exceeded my greatest expectations. It's explosive, extravagant, whole-hearted and passionate. I love the way Africans worship. Monday night worship is supposed to last one hour, but often goes for the whole three hours of the school night and further. I can't tell you how many breakthroughs happen in that kind of glory and presence.

People have been healed, delivered, filled with the Holy Spirit, given revelations, gotten clarity about their future, gotten huge downloads of God ideas for projects, businesses, and the list goes on and on. Things can happen in one session of glorious worship that could take weeks, months, and even years to accomplish.

The prophetic has also grown and become a foundational rock in our community. Everyone learns how to prophesy and we encourage our students to "practice the prophetic" on a regular basis and live a prophetic lifestyle.

We've built a community of love and family at BASSM-C as well. Community and mutual support are important core values in Africa and I've never experienced anything like it. No one can go hungry, be sick, or go through pain or difficulty alone. Everyone takes care of everyone and is there for everyone. People value time together, meals together and fellowship just for the sake of fellowship. Unlike Western culture, relationship and community are valued above accomplishing tasks.

The school is more than just a place to learn about God and the supernatural. We have yearly Love Feasts where the staff and interns pour out on the students. In an idea adapted from BASSM, we set up stations for people to receive love and ministry. There's a foot washing station where students wash each other's feet. There's a room for prophetic presbytery, where students receive loads of prophetic words to encourage them and launch them into their destiny. There's a massage room where people can be loved on with the healing touch and great soaking music. And there's a room where we take people on "trips to heaven." This is a guided session where we lead people into a God encounter – led by someone well experienced in having God encounters and entering into His presence.[3]

It's become one of the great events at BASSM-C and guests love to attend. Some end up being students after experiencing a Love Feast. We also have Friday night fellowships once or twice a month. We either have glorious worship that we don't have to worry about stopping for class, or we have family fun nights where we play games, eat, watch movies, laugh, and spend quality fun time together.

We have trips to the beach at least once a year. For some of the students, it's the first time they've gone to the beach. It's only thirty minutes away from Buea, but many of them have never seen the ocean. In a legalistic religious culture, I love to teach people that God is fun. He's not spooky spiritual all the time. He likes to have fun and enjoy His kids. I know He gets as much pleasure from us splashing in the ocean and playing soccer together as He does when we're praying for the sick.

In our fifth year of BASSM-C, we began to outgrow our building. By that time, we had launched a second and a third year program and had more students than ever. Alumni also enjoy coming back for worship so Monday nights are packed. We began searching the city for a new building to house us. The search lasted too long without any success.

By year six, Monday night worship was so packed that people ended up worshipping outside. I have pictures of people kneeling and lying prostrate on the front porch and others standing with their arms raised in complete abandon in the front yard. I love it that people get so lost in worship that they don't even care that they're outside the building. They still get caught up in the presence of God.

But it was hot, stuffy and crowded inside. We could barely dance because there were too many people in the room. We increased our efforts toward finding a new building and had teams of staff and students going all over town, looking at buildings. Nothing was large enough to house us.

Me and my Transformation Center team traveled to Lagos, Nigeria for a Randy Clark conference. We've partnered with Lapis Lazuli ministries, the hosts of the conference, to bring sozo (inner healing sessions) and the message of the Kingdom to Nigeria. After the conference, we were to do sozos to usher people into freedom and to help train new inner healers.

While in Nigeria, I got phone calls from the staff in Cameroon saying they had found a building. It would seat double the number of people (we could squeeze eighty into our current building). It was located further down in the heart of the city and was on the main road. It was also brand new. The drawback was it had two floors of open space and we would have to build out offices. I had seen the building before and it was modern and well-appointed so I told them to get it.

Meeting after meeting with the landlords fell through. They wanted too much money. There was a dispute over who owned the building and whether it could be rented and who the money would go to (common problems with land and real estate there). The door kept slamming shut in our face.

They staff finally said they believed it wasn't God and that we needed to search elsewhere. I kept pushing for that nice, new, modern building. The diva missionary wanted those huge windows and nice marble floors.

I went home for Christmas that year and a few days into my break, got a message from my staff.

We found THE building for us. It's a miracle and definitely the building God has just for us. It's perfect!

It was located on the main road in Bueatown, a quaint village at the base of the mountain. Kingsley, our worship director, was the one leading the search and so he prayed about our new building often. One night, he saw this building in a dream and God told him it was ours. He told us about it in staff meeting, but others told him the building was occupied by several businesses. We joke and laugh a lot in our staff meetings, so he got a good ribbing about his prophetic gift being off and him having eru dreams (the Cameroonian equivalent of our pizza dreams).

He kept thinking about the building and the dream and one day stopped by to check on it. He discovered that the current tenants were moving out and the building would be available in a couple months.

The building is a historic landmark, built by German colonizers back in the late 1800's. It was the first cinema hall (movie house) in Cameroon and therefore is very large with high ceilings and a balcony. Over the years, it's been a church, ministry school, and has housed a few businesses.

When they sent me pictures of this "perfect building," I thought they'd lost their minds. It was a WRECK! It looked like a construction zone and was filthy. They joked that I needed to see it through the eyes of the spirit and get a revelation from God about it being our building. Kingsley reminded me of his dream and begged me to trust him that everything would be fine. I begged him to go back and negotiate for that other shiny, brand new building they had found.

I finally decided to trust my staff – my "kids" who I've raised to be full of faith and vision. We signed papers on the "new" building. I'll spare you the details of the fights with the landlord to make the repairs, after he'd made so many grandiose promises about all he was going to do. The building turned out better than I expected.

This color and design obsessed, diva missionary had the best time picking out paint colors, curtains, and new pictures. We still have a LOT of upgrades to make and things to fix, but that'll happen a little bit at a time.

The new building seats five times as many people as the previous hall and the cost isn't twice as much. We have a separate office space behind the balcony so the Transformation Center (inner healing and counseling) can be isolated from other school activities. We have a huge staff office, a large library, a sweet little prayer room and administrative offices.

We hosted our first graduation at our own hall at the end of Year 6 and it was packed to capacity with almost 400 people. Every graduation is glorious, but this one was extra special because we were hosting it at home. Even though it still needs work, we all love our new hall and look forward to hosting many more graduations, worship events, and conferences.

God has done small and big miracles over the years – if one can categorize the size of a miracle. Many of them are personal expressions of His love for me and demonstrate His care for my unique personality.

One example is one of my staff members, Randolf, the youngest among us. Randolf graduated from Bethel Atlanta Cameroon in the third year. He and a friend "snuck" into school. I didn't realize he wasn't eligible to attend until almost halfway through, when he showed up in his high school uniform. I fussed at him, that we didn't allow high school students to attend and that he should come back after graduation. He begged to be able to finish the school year. I allowed him to stay on the condition that his high school grades didn't drop. Back then, I considered him a silly kid, which he was.

After graduation, he disappeared for a year and then came back when we launched the second year program. He had matured greatly during that time and had taught himself how to play the keyboard by ear and watching YouTube videos.

I have to admit to being frustrated that many church musicians in Cameroon stick to the basic chords with no flavor or extra spice. I love jazz and missed the complexity of jazz and gospel music lost in the limited 1,4,5 chords widely played there.

The first time I heard Randolf play, I was shocked. He sounded like a jazz musician and fed a musical hunger that had been growing since my time in Cameroon. When he realized how much I loved his playing, he threw himself into studying more. I gave him tons of music from my extensive collection, and before my eyes, he's grown into an accomplished keyboardist.

To add to that, one of my friends and her husband donated a high quality keyboard to the school – the kind you see on the stages of famous performers. We shipped it over and surprised Randolf. I love to watch the video where he falls on the ground shouting the first time he saw it. He composed a song right there on the spot to thank my friends for such an amazing gift.

Randolf also dreams of opening his own sound company one day. He went to "YouTube University" to study sound and designed a sound system for our five times bigger hall. We shipped the order from Amazon.com over with Mr. Ehabe. The first time I heard the new keyboard and the new sound system, along with Randolf's first year student friends – an amazing bass player and drummer – I was in HEAVEN! I love live music and used to spend a lot of time in many of Atlanta's live music venues. Being in Cameroon, I missed that part of my life. And now God was giving it to me, through my kids I was raising to live their dreams.

That first day, my boys played and I sang. All the worship songs I had written twenty years prior in my days at Intercessors for Christ came rushing back to my memory. So did all my prophetic words about bringing down heaven with amazing worship and recording albums that would go global. Me, Randolf and his friends had a worship session and I taught them a few of the songs. I know we'll write new music together too. Maybe soon, Bethel Atlanta Cameroon will have a worship album with our own, unique sound created as a fusion of West African, American jazz and gospel nuances.

I go into this much detail to show you how much God loves us and how much He cares about what we care about. He knows how much I love music and cares that good worship is important to me. He knows I need jazz and gospel chords in my life and also a great sound system rather than the hollow, tinny, ringing or buzzing sound systems I've tried to endure in Cameroon.

Daddy God is okay with me being a diva missionary and He takes care of my needs, but also cares about my wants. He's gifted me with many impromptu trips to the beach, two trips to South Africa (one with an overnight layover in my Nairobi with Rosie!), gifts of a Bose mini speaker and Beats headphones, (may seem silly, but these items are essential to an avid music lover!) a ridiculously expensive trip to South Beach in Miami with my best friend from college, an endless supply of gourmet, dark chocolate from everyone who knows my addiction, and a steady supply of Teavana (ridiculously expensive gourmet tea with expensive infusers to prepare it in).

Right now, I'm sitting at a beach – my favorite place in the world – writing this book because I thought a thought that I needed to go somewhere beautiful and peaceful to finish writing the first draft. I didn't even pray it out loud to God, just thought it. And then I mentioned it to my writing partner and she said she happened to have a free week at her timeshare. That's the God Zone! A free vacation at Panama City beach, writing about the God Zone.

No matter how long I live in the God Zone, the miracles still stun me. It's amazing to live a life loved by a good, good Father. The God Zone is a beautifully, miraculous place of provision, favor, health, protection, and most of all, lavish love.

I could go on and on with the list of things God does to feed the diva side of me. When I gave up my doctor job, doctor car, doctor house, doctor vacations, and doctor salary to go live in Cameroon, God was watching. He makes sure He gives me treats and surprises and cares about the special things that bring me joy and make me feel like His loved, spoiled daughter. I really am His favorite!

The God Zone is more than just supernatural provision for His vision to build the Kingdom. It's also about His babygirl, Sherri, and the things that matter to her.

Even with all the amazing things going on at the school and in my life, I was about to enter into one of the darkest seasons ever, rivaled only by my divorce. It was only God that gave me the grace to fight my way out of it.

[3]*Experiencing the Heavenly Realms: Keys to Accessing Supernatural Encounters*, Judy Franklin and Beni Johnson, 2016

Fifteen

Looking back, I realize it took me a while to bounce back from Ernestine's death. Longer than I care to admit.

One of my favorite things about being a Christian is enjoying an intimate relationship with God. I love to wake up every morning and see myself sitting on His lap. He covers my face with kisses and sings His special morning song – the one just for me – as I sit and soak up His love. We talk about EVERYTHING – not in religious prayers with thee's and thou's and quoted Scriptures, but I talk to Him intimately, like a best friend.

After Ernestine died, something in me died, and it affected our intimacy. That next year, me and my then ministry partner/housemate brought home a very sick baby from an orphanage where we served. I fell in love with him and wanted to adopt him. And then we found out that what we thought was a temporary, curable illness was actually a rare, incurable brain disease.

I have to admit I backed away from helping her with his care. Baby Elliot was very sick and my ministry partner took many trips back and forth to

Yaoundé to save his life. We prayed and warred over him, prophesied and declared a long, healthy life for him. But one day, just like Ernestine, we got the phone call that Baby Elliot had died and was dancing with Jesus in heaven. Something in me died a little more and my intimacy with God was even more deeply affected.

I didn't realize how much until my good friend, Felicia Murrell, came over on a mission trip. She's a gifted inner healer and counselor and had become a regular visitor at Bethel Atlanta Cameroon. One evening, she sat in my parlor with me and a few other close ones who had been most affected by Ernestine and Baby Elliot's deaths. With gentle, soul digging questions, and heart piercing words, she helped us realize we were offended at God. She prayed for Him to heal our hearts and restore our intimacy with and trust in Him.

Over the next year, I became very intentional about getting my relationship with God completely healed. I live off of our intimacy. It's not optional for me. Without deep, intimate relationship with Him on a daily basis, I'm not happy and whole, and function as a much lesser version of myself. I was still teaching, preaching, worshipping, and interceding and imparting during that entire time, but my heart and my intimacy with Him were damaged. And intimacy is one of the most important components to living in the God Zone.

I wanted *us* back and planned to do everything I could to make that happen (It's never Him that walks away from intimacy. Just us.). Over the course of a year, I allowed God to heal my heart. I returned to the place where I sat on His lap every morning and talked and laughed with Him while washing the dishes. I once again looked like a madwoman walking down the dusty roads of Buea, engaged in full-on conversation with Him as if He were physically walking next to me. We were *back*.

And then the enemy struck again. I knew from the kind of attack that he was trying to destroy my intimacy and therefore my ministry for good.

Bessie, my Transformation Center director, and her mother graduated from the very first year of BASSM-C. Mami Evelyn was one of the few older people that attended the school. Most of our students are college aged or in their early thirties. Bessie was an intern the first year and has been on staff ever since. She eventually became my roommate and we grew closer and closer. Family being what it is in Africa, I grew close to Bessie's mom.

She became my Cameroonian mother. She cooked my favorite dishes for me when Bessie told her I had a craving. Every time I traveled, she made chin chin – a Cameroonian treat of little strips of shortbread cookies – to make sure I had snacks on my way back to America. She respected, honored, and loved me in a very special way. I always told her if I married a

Cameroonian, she'd stand in for my mother and dance at my wedding.

So you can imagine my horror when she was diagnosed with breast cancer in January of 2013. After the diagnosis, we began walking through the nightmare of cancer treatment in Cameroon. I tease Bessie that Mami Evelyn loved me the most because when she woke up from her mastectomy, it was my name she called first. The surgery was VERY poorly done and they didn't check for lymph nodes or even get good cancer margins. The biopsy specimen for diagnosis was insufficient, so we weren't even sure of the type of cancer we were treating. It was so frustrating being a doctor during this time because I could see everything that was being done wrong, and I'd try to discuss it with her caregivers, but they'd shrug and give me a look like, "This isn't America."

We had to drive to Douala for radiation and chemotherapy – that is, when the radiation machine wasn't broken down. Douala is only five degrees cooler than hell itself, with bad traffic, so those were difficult journeys.

Mami Evelyn was in remission for a short while, and then the cancer reared its ugly head with spread to the liver. Again, I'll spare you the details. We prayed, warred, prophesied life, but on September 21, 2014, two days after our first KLA graduation, Mami Evelyn went home to be with Jesus.

Our whole Bethel Atlanta Cameroon community was devastated. We had the KLA graduation, had her funeral, and then a week later had to start Year 5 of a school of supernatural ministry. "Heal the sick, raise the dead" seemed very hollow in those days. Our staff is very close knit, so Bessie's mom's death affected us all and cut to the core of our faith in everything we were teaching and living.

I know we're not supposed to get upset with God when things like this happen. I can quote whole sections of Bill Johnson's two-part series, *How to Overcome Disappointment* – the messages he shared about the weeks surrounding his father's death from cancer. I didn't want to lose any ground in my intimacy with God, so I decided to fight hard not to get offended again.

I went through another ministry divorce during that time with my ministry partner. I won't go into any details, but it was a heart-wrenching, painful loss. Relationship is high on my list of core values, so I do everything within my power to preserve it, especially with close relationships. With both ministry divorces, I met with my leadership at Bethel Atlanta and trusted inner healers for counsel. I'm not a person that breaks relationship easily, but all my advisors and leaders agreed I had to let go. No matter how much it hurt.

Three months later after Mami Evelyn's death, the brother of two of our first-year graduates, former YA members and close friends, died. We had been fighting for his life against a mysterious illness for two years (Those familiar with witchcraft in Africa know what I mean by mysterious illness.). A few weeks later, my uncle died, and then the next month, the mother of a first/second year BASSM-C graduate died.

And then the next month, my grandfather died.

And then my Dad's younger sister was diagnosed with advanced stomach cancer. And then one of our student's brother was killed in a bus accident along with many other students from a local school. The pandemonium, mourning, and carnage of bodies piled up at the mortuary that day are forever burned in my memory.

And then I found out the little girl I wanted to adopt – that had a room in my house full of clothes, shoes, toys, and books – was unadoptable. I had fallen in love with her on my many trips to the orphanage and had spent a lot of time with her. I had been able to bring her home on many school holidays. She loved to sing, loved to read books with me, loved to dance and actually looked like me. In my heart, she was mine.

I haven't shared my battle with infertility during my marriage, or how I'd closed off my heart to children for so many years, or how this little girl opened my heart back up and made a part of me live and dream about being a mommy again. A month after I submitted the paperwork to adopt her, Cameroon passed a law that no longer allowed foreign adoptions because of problems they were having with child trafficking. It felt like that news killed the last surviving fragment of my heart.

But it continued. My aunt died in June. Bessie's younger sister's husband died of a mysterious illness in August and she became a widow and single mother at the age of twenty-six – not even a year after losing her mother.

In October, one of my spiritual daughters, who had graduated from first year and KLA and had served as an intern, got married had a baby. The baby died because of criminally poor medical management a few hours after she was born. My daughter, Katy, and I sat on her bed together not even two hours after her baby died. I cried when she whispered that the baby was named after me – Sherrilynn. She lost a second baby not even a year later.

Through all this, I clung to God with everything in me. I was determined not to move my heart away from His again, but I was overwhelmed by all the losses. I asked Him one day why all these people around me were dying. He reminded me that the average life expectancy in Cameroon is fifty-seven years, as compared to seventy-nine in America. When you live as a part of the community and they become family, those aren't statistics on a World Health Organization webpage. Those are mothers, brother, sisters, daughters, and close friends.

I appreciated Him answering in a way that made sense, but it didn't make the pain of the losses any lighter. It put a greater determination in my heart to bring revival to Cameroon and the nations of Africa. It gave me a greater drive to see the miraculous on a regular basis.

I also started to become frustrated with the difficulties of living in Cameroon. Missionaries have a certain extra grace to be able to tolerate living conditions less than the standard they're used to. I became a full-time missionary at the age of forty, after living as a doctor's daughter, and then as a doctor myself. There was a certain type of lifestyle I was accustomed to. In spite of God making sure I had all the possible diva luxuries available, it was still challenging. Every single day.

It aggravated me that much of the underdevelopment issues in Cameroon could be fixed over time if there wasn't so much government corruption. I could launch into a whole discourse about how colonization and the spirit of poverty can destroy a nation and its people, but that's for another book.

I told God I needed a new apartment, or a house that wasn't up a quarter mile footpath of rocks and dirt (I'd moved off the main road because of the noise and constant flow of unexpected, uninvited visitors). I needed a car. I needed more frequent trips out of Cameroon and away from the death and poverty that was affecting my soul's well-being.

I needed to heal from all the deaths and stop feeling unsafe, unprotected, and uncovered. I needed to stop being afraid every time the phone rang or every time one of my kids said they had a headache or a fever or said they were traveling somewhere by bus. I needed to believe in this supernatural life I had given up everything to teach.

Let me pause here and bring some balance. It wasn't only death and loss we were experiencing. We saw many healings on our student outreaches. Many students and graduates adopted a lifestyle of outreach and came back with testimonies of healings, deliverance, life changing prophetic words and words of knowledge, relationship restoration, financial miracles and all sorts of other miraculous God stuff. I'm learning to stop focusing on what I may feel God isn't doing and practice gratitude for what He *IS* doing. Since I told you about all the losses, let me tell you a few of the many miracles.

In the midst of all these deaths, our community experienced its first resurrection. Pastor Sako (the first person who greeted me when I walked in the door on my very first trip to Cameroon) was a student the third year after BASSM-C was established. He participated in KLA, became an intern, and finally an Outreach Coordinator on our staff. He loves, lives, and breathes outreach and ministers wherever he goes.

He made a trip to a small village in the Northwest and was carrying on a crusade – preaching, prophesying, and doing deliverance. He had just cast out a demon when two young men carried a woman in and laid her on the floor.

He asked, "What's wrong with her?"

"She's dead," was their reply.

Pastor Sako has an amazing sense of humor and I love to hear him tell this story. He panicked. He's been preaching and ministering on stage in front of the whole village and everyone has seen him do miracles. Now there's a dead woman lying on the floor in front of him and many expectant eyes are on him.

He did what any of us would do in this situation. He prayed in tongues for about an hour straight, trying to encourage himself and find some faith, somewhere. Finally, he decided to go for it. He asked a woman to lay hands on the dead woman's stomach (I teach them that men shouldn't lay hands on women's chests or stomachs).

I've seen the video from this point forward. The camera is focused on the dead woman's chest showing the praying woman's hand on her belly. Pastor Sako can be heard in the background, rebuking death. All of a sudden, the woman's hand jumps off the stomach and you can see her feet running out the door. She later told Pastor Sako that she felt the woman's heart start beating and it scared her, so she ran.

After a few seconds, the dead woman starts moving her head back and forth. I've watched the video too many times – I have to admit – to chase away doubt and unbelief. A resurrection is a crazy, unbelievable miracle and I couldn't get my doctor brain wrapped around it, even though I've been reading Bible stories about people being resurrected from the dead all my life!

When watching the video, I stare at her chest, seeing that there's absolutely no rise and fall to signify she's breathing, even when her head is rocking back and forth and her arms are moving. All of a sudden, she takes a dramatic, gasping breath and her chest begins to rise and fall.

It perplexes my doctor brain every time I watch it. I can't understand how her head starts moving a full ten or so seconds before she starts breathing. But I guess the miraculous doesn't have to follow the laws of medical science. Pretty soon, she gets up and stumbles around confused. Pastor Sako prays for her and the video ends.

She brought him a sack of potatoes the next day, to thank him for bringing her back to life. Food is often given as offering rather than money in poor villages. Pastor Sako also has videos of two deaf women hearing for the first time in their lives.

Another miracle happened for one of our graduates. Bih had a terrible sickle cell flare during that time. She had sepsis and pneumonia and was in and out of the hospital and didn't get to participate in KLA as she had planned. We drove to her parents' house in Kumba (another hot like you've gone to hell town about an hour away from Buea) to pray for her.

I know what impending death looks like and death was sitting in the corner of the parlor the whole time we visited Bih. We and many others prayed for her and now she's married and living in North Carolina, getting her Masters in Nursing. I remember peeking in the window to see her beautifully dressed, vibrant and alive on the day of her traditional wedding (it was too crowded to get inside for the ceremony part). The difference between the way she looked that day death was looming, waiting to snatch her, and on that wedding day could only be described as a miracle.

Since I mentioned the first resurrection, I should go ahead and tell of the second. Pastor Sako came to staff meeting one day, sad and tired because he had been up the night before, praying for a four-year old that had died of a mysterious illness the day before. Unfortunately, that's a common story in Cameroon that I've heard too many times. A child wakes up in the morning, complains of a headache, goes to school, then comes home and dies in the evening.

Pastor Sako and some students prayed for the child for hours, but she didn't wake up. I don't know what keeps him going and praying for the sick and the dead, but he does. A few weeks later, he was in the hospital visiting a relative and found out about another tragedy. A woman was wailing loudly in the hallway, as Africans do when someone dies. He approached the family and asked what had happened. He learned that this was the sixth child this woman had lost. Each of her children were born, lived sickly to the age of eight months, and then died.

He asked the family if he could pray. One uncle told him not to bother – this was the way things went for this family. Pastor Sako persisted and they agreed to let him pray.

He prayed for one hour straight with no results. He started getting nervous and discouraged as more and more people gathered to watch. Finally, the Holy Spirit told him to give the baby mouth-to-mouth. Pastor Sako has never been trained in CPR, so did what he'd seen in movies and on television. After a few breaths, the baby coughed and then cried.

I can only imagine the shock and rejoicing that happened in that hospital. I have a picture and a short video in my phone of that baby to remind me of God's goodness and His miraculous resurrection power.

It's not only miraculous healings and resurrections. God has been faithful to reveal Himself to me as Jehovah Jireh, just as I asked Him to before I started the school. There's no real way to reconcile what comes in through donations with what goes out in expenses, other than to say it's a miracle. We've always had more than enough to run the school and for me to live on. Always. There have been some moments when we were down to the bottom of our bank account, wondering what to do next, and then a check comes in the mail – just in time.

Again, I think God, Jesus, and the Holy Spirit have a great time in heaven, watching us start to sweat just a little, and then they spring a surprise, out-of-nowhere donation on us at the perfect moment. I've started to play along with them, and instead of freaking out and panicking, I wait like an excited child at Christmas, watching to see from which direction the miracle will come.

God has never let us down when it comes to provision and finances. He has always provided everything we've needed and even for our wants. As our dreams grow bigger and our needs more, I've had a few, almost freak out moments. Then I whisper to God, "You don't deserve my fear. You deserve my absolute trust because You're a faithful Father and You've been so miraculously and generously good." I rebuke fear and wait for the miracle to come. And it comes. Every…single…time.

In this difficult season, when the tension between miracles, promises, and losses was affecting my soul, I again got restless for more. I wanted something more and something new. At the same time, I was too tired and discouraged to reach for it. I whispered prayers on a regular basis, telling God that most of all, I needed Him to help me stay close to Him and not allow my internal reality to be affected by external circumstances.

I cried out to Him as often as I needed to, trusting Him to keep me, keep us, and keep Bethel Atlanta Cameroon. I also trusted Him to meet my heart's desire for something more.

Sixteen

After that season of losses and difficulties, I was burnt out and tired. I kept telling God I needed to get away. My whole life revolved around Bethel Atlanta Cameroon. I was either in Cameroon, being Aunty Sherri/Mommy Sherri/Director, or in Atlanta, raising money and planning for the school. I cried out to God for someplace I could go just to be Sherri, the girl.

For some reason, my heart started stirring to go to Kenya again. I had fallen deeply in love with the nation the first time I went and when I thought about the place I wanted to go to relax, I thought of the coffee shops, the great restaurants, the shopping, and the beauty and feel of Nairobi.

I asked God for money to go. I edited a book and got enough for a plane ticket. Thank God for Unoma Nwankor, whose author grind has funded many of my international trips (Please read her books and be a blessing to her for her being such a blessing to me!).

I started to book the plane ticket, but then thought, *so I'm gonna fly to Kenya and do what? Sit on the curb and beg once I get there? I have NO money to spend while I'm there. I want to go on safari. I want to drink lattes and gourmet tea every day. I want to eat Ethiopian and Indian food.*

I decided that going to Kenya was out of the question because I wouldn't have enough money to enjoy it. I put the idea away and determined to spend some time in the Word and worship to get myself feeling better.

The next morning I woke up and was like – *I gotta get out of here!*

My staff was running KLA, our third summer program, and I was actually wondering why I had come back from the US for it. They had grown to the point where they no longer needed me to do it. That made me feel great – proud of who they've become – but it also made me feel restless and itchy for a new adventure. I had been itching for about two years, but now the itching was unbearable.

God asked me, ***"How much would you need to enjoy Kenya?"***

I thought about it for a second and said, "$600 more dollars. No, $800. Well, since you're asking, I want to have a great time and not worry about money. I need $1,000. Please?"

I didn't have anywhere I could get that much money in a short period. There were no editing jobs on the horizon and I still had my issue with pride and not wanting to ask anyone for anything. Especially not a frivolous vacation just for the sake of me enjoying a latte. I put the thought aside and went on with my day.

A few hours later, I got a Vox audio message from my mom. "I left you a message two days ago. You might want to listen to it." I had seen the notification when the message came through on the walkie–talkie message app that's become a lifeline for me as a missionary, but hadn't had time to listen to it yet, which was unusual for me.

I listened to her message. "Hey, Sherri. You got a check in the mail. You won't believe what it's from." She went on to explain there was a settlement from a business transaction from something that happened five years ago. I didn't even know there was a class action lawsuit or that I had been involved in it.

Her voice continued, "Get this. It's $1300…"

I dropped the phone and screamed, "I'm going to Kenya!!!"

There are times God really shocks me with His love. I felt so loved and cared for in that moment. He chose to come through in a way that made no logical sense and was completely unexpected. I got online and booked my flight.

I started looking for places to stay. Rosie's mom had moved to Canada as a diplomat and Rosie was living with her aunt. I looked at several Airbnb spots and sent them to Rosie to make sure I'd at least be somewhat close to where she lived. I picked one with good ratings that looked gorgeous and realized how much it would cut into my money. I should have asked for more, since He was in such a generous mood!

I wrote the leaders of the Kingdom Academy ministry school I had visited and bonded with on my first trip. I'd been Facebook friends with the leaders since and we kept up with what was going on in each other's ministries. I emailed Brittanie who had moved from that village outside Mombasa to Nairobi. And a few years back, I found out that Apostle Peterson had gotten remarried to a Kenyan woman and was living in Nairobi as well. I sent him an email and he said he couldn't wait to see me.

Me and Brittanie wrote back and forth and I told her the area I had found the Airbnb in and hoped it would be near her so we could spend some time together.

Brittanie wrote back, "You can stay at my place for free if you'd like. It's really nice. You'd have your own room with a bathroom and access to my kitchen and living room. I'll send you the Airbnb link so you can see the house. But you don't need to pay…"

The God Zone. I'll never live anywhere else.

I wrote Rosie and she said Brittanie's house was about eight minutes from hers. This was starting to feel good. Like destiny.

My friend and fellow missionary, Felecia Foster, kept telling me to keep my heart wide open about Kenya. "This trip is gonna be a game changer. It's going to change everything about your whole life. Be open to whatever God says and does. Okay?"

We Vox pretty much every day and she had been walking me through the dark season with love and encouraging words. Not sure how she didn't get tired of me whining and being fearful and faithless all the time.

"Girl, I'm going on vacation. I ain't thinking about a game changer or anything like that. I just need to rest and drink some lattes."

My mouth was saying that, but my heart was leaping. I felt it, too. Something was about to change drastically and it had everything to do with this miraculous trip to Kenya.

I can't explain how it felt when I touched down at Kenyatta International Airport, hugged my sweet Rosie, and started driving to Brittanie's house. I can't explain my emotions the first few days of being in Kenya. It feels like a completely different world from Cameroon. The spiritual atmosphere is different. I felt free – like I could breathe, think, and be creative.

I could walk to the mall down the street from Brittanie's house. I met Rosie there, planning to go to Art Caffe for a latte, but saw the sweetest thing – Melvin's Moments Tea House. This little teahouse is a bright, open space with comfortable chairs and modern décor at the bottom of a huge atrium that extended to the top of the mall in all glass windows. There was a perfect breeze and it was perfect for people watching and catching the vibe of Nairobi. I ordered a hibiscus ginger tea and it was heavenly. The place felt like me...

We went to an arts festival and I enjoyed watching the young artists milling about with their well-styled, natural hair and chic African clothing. I didn't feel the weight of poverty and the desperation for survival. These people were on a quest for creativity, arts, enlightenment, and enjoyment.

Nairobi felt like an African Atlanta to me. I started to talk to God about it. It was a crazy thought, but what if I moved there? What would it be like to start a school in Nairobi? To be able to reach out to young creatives? To live in Africa, but be able to go to tea houses and coffee shops and malls? Within days, I was cooking gourmet, healthy meals and walking four miles a day at a nearby sports track. I was singing and dancing around the house, laughing a lot and feeling something I hadn't felt in a while...hope.

After a few days, I wrote in my journal.

Okay, I'm finally able to admit it feels like the grace has lifted for me being in Cameroon. You know how much I love BA-Cameroon and my kids and even Cameroon itself, but it's wearing on my soul. I can't live there most of the year anymore.

Being in Nairobi makes me realize there's a different Africa. One filled with hope and progress and pride and...life. Being here wouldn't feel like missions. It feels like Atlanta. You had to persuade me to move to Cameroon, but You wouldn't have to persuade me to move here. In fact, I'm begging You for it.

I could still go to Cameroon on a regular basis, but my staff can run the school. But I feel guilty about abandoning the work. No, that's not true. I've developed a work that can sustain itself with me coming at times to pour into it. I want BA Cameroon to succeed and thrive. But I don't want to die in the process.

You brought me here for a reason. I hope it's because I could move here. Are You asking me or am I asking You? I refuse to feel guilty for wanting more. I'm an Atlanta girl. I love art and beauty and fun and ambiance and neat coffee shops and progressive people.

You're good. You love me. You know exactly what I need. I put my trust in You. Show me what to do. Heal my heart while I'm here. Tell me what to do. I'm open. I'm here. I'm Yours.

Love You...

I put the thoughts to rest and decided to forget it all and just have fun. I no longer wanted to go on safari. I wanted to drink tea or lattes, eat good, healthy food, exercise and enjoy the people, relax, and *be*. I wanted to be Sherri in my African Atlanta and enjoy.

But the question kept sneaking into my mind. Would God let me move to Nairobi? The thought caused so much hope and happiness, I could hardly contain it.

That Sunday, I went to Eagles' Nest church with Rosie. I enjoyed the worship and the word and went up to greet the leaders afterwards. Pastor Niyi joked that it was time for me to relocate and build a Bethel Atlanta School in Nairobi. His wife, Pastor Esther, gave me a prophetic word. It was long and detailed, but she basically said that my season in Cameroon was over and it was time to begin building a work in a new country. I thought I came to Nairobi on vacation, but God had a completely different reason for me coming, to give me a new assignment. Kenya was a strategic place to build a BASSM and God was bringing me there and to other nations in Africa.

I was overwhelmed. I wasn't on vacation? God brought me here to change my whole life? It wasn't me that wanted to move to Nairobi, but God was actually spearheading the whole thing?

My heart filled with a strange sense of fearful excitement. I was going to get to move to Nairobi to start a school? I was going to get to live in my African Atlanta?

Of course, Rosie was excited. A few days later, I went to her house to hang with her and another graduate of Kingdom Academy, Loise. Rosie wanted us to dream about Bethel Atlanta Kenya, but I still wasn't sure. I wanted God to confirm it. I didn't want to dream about something that I wanted, but that He didn't want. I had gotten one prophetic word – an amazing one – but I'd never made any huge life decisions on one word. I needed more than that to think about starting a school in a whole new nation in Africa.

Rosie was chattering about how exciting it was going to be and thinking of where we would hold classes. She was in full-on dream mode.

I stopped her. "Rosie, I don't want to have this conversation. I need to be sure this is God first. You're getting me all excited and happy, but if this isn't God, then I'll be disappointed. Let's just wait until I'm sure it's Him and then we can talk about it and plan everything out. I need at least two confirmations and I need them from people I trust outside of Kenya. Then I can be sure and then we can talk. Okay?"

Rosie was visibly disappointed, but said she understood. I had just finished a big cup of tea, so got up and went to the bathroom. When I got back, there was a typed Vox message waiting for me from Felicia Murrell.

I woke up thinking about you. Have you considered moving to Kenya? Starting ministry there? It came to me so quick this morning. Cameroon is going strong. You have a team there to handle it. You could replicate ministry in Kenya...

They are ready to continue the work without you being there. And you're ready for something new. You're a pioneer. You're denying your true self by staying there. You've just finished Year 6. This coming year is Year 7. That's completion...

I screamed.

I felt the Holy Spirit say, "***That's confirmation number one. How many did you say you need"?***

I was floored. Felicia is one of the most trusted prophetic voices in my life. And the timing of it was uncanny. I told Rosie and Loise. Rosie teased that I should have trusted her prophetic voice, but if I needed God to confirm it from others, He would. She launched right back into her dreaming and planning. I didn't hear much. I was too shocked.

This was happening...

A few days later, I was supposed to go somewhere in the morning, but felt like the Holy Spirit wanted me to stay home and spend some time with Him. I knew there was something He wanted to say, but I was a little restless and nervous. I listened for a while, but then started finding ways to distract myself. I needed to call my friend, Alero. I had met her on my trip to Nigeria. Much more on her later.

I had just read her new book, *Reformer's Arise*, a treatise about raising young revivalists in the nations of Africa to invade and conquer the 7 Mountains of Influence. I'd thoroughly enjoyed reading it on the flight over from Cameroon. She was speaking my language. I wanted to give her feedback and discuss me editing it.

A few minutes into the conversation with Alero, we switched from talking about the book to talking about how to actually raise up reformers in Africa. We launched into a full-blown, prophetic conversation about bringing young Africans together from many countries, giving them foundational Kingdom training and then releasing them to invade and conquer the 7 Mountains. I felt that strong bond I felt from the first moment I met her and knew this was a divine connection.

Alero then started speaking into my life. She said I'm a pioneer and a visionary and I'm called to the nations of Africa and not just Cameroon. She talked about her being a visionary and how it used to make her feel guilty when she started something and then five years later was ready to move on to the next thing. The Holy Spirit had to show her she was a visionary and she shouldn't feel guilty. Her pioneering cycle was five years and she shouldn't feel guilty when it was time to move on.

My mouth fell open. I told her, "Wow, God is speaking to me through you. I'm going through exactly that right now." She had given words to the intense guilt I was feeling over considering leaving my beloved work in Cameroon. She encouraged me for a while, speaking to the apostolic call on my life and encouraging me that I was called to many nations and I wasn't to get stuck in one place.

"I was hoping you'd come to Nigeria next, but if God is saying Kenya, so be it." She invited me to come to London where she lived to discuss more about building a formal structure around raising reformers and revivalists in the nations of Africa. I got off the phone, completely floored.

I've learned that God has so much personality and He relates to us in a way that fits our personality. I'm snarky and mouthy and often, He jokes with me and gets funny and sarcastic just like me.

I wasn't surprised when the Holy Spirit said, ***"That's two confirmations, from people outside of Kenya. How many do you need or is that enough? Because I can send more. Just tell Me how many..."***

Everywhere I went, I found myself seated with Kingdom people, having apostolic conversations. Everyone told me about the strategies to take the continent of Africa. They said, "If you take Kenya in the East, then you get with it Burundi, Rwanda, Uganda, and Tanzania. Then you have to take South African and maybe one other country in Southern Africa."

I have no idea why, but Botswana instantly jumped into my thoughts.

"Then you have to take Nigeria in the West and with it comes Ghana and the smaller surrounding countries. Central Africa is another challenge. And then if you decide to take Northern Africa, you must take Egypt."

Something deep inside me stirred. I remembered some recent prophetic words about an apostolic call on my life. I cringed every time I got them. Apostolic – that's such a big word for such a little girl. But as they outlined strategies for taking a continent, deep was calling unto deep and my vision was expanding by the minute.

I remembered a prophetic word I had gotten that I was riding on a hot air balloon over the nations of Africa. There were different colors on the balloon, each color representing a different nation. As I flew over the different countries, the people recognized me and ran out to welcome me. I brought them great gifts and deep revelation from the Kingdom that would bring revival and change.

I remembered the visions I had when I first started praying for Cameroon. Cameroon was on fire, covered in glory, but that glory eventually spilled over into the other nations of Africa.

Was it time to leave my sweet little comfort zone in Cameroon and expand to another nation? Or other nations?

The more meetings I had, the more my heart swelled. And the more I was ready to dig and lay roots in Kenya. But how was I going to tell my kids at home? And what would my leadership at Bethel Atlanta think?

Seventeen

I finally got up the courage to text my leadership team at Bethel Atlanta. It took me a week, because honestly, I was scared of what they would think. A new country? The whole continent of Africa? If I shared my dreams with them, would they think I was crazy and stressed and tired? Would they ask me to come home for a break and some inner healing until I came back to my senses?

Lindy Hale, who always texts me with the perfect prophetic words and prayers texted back her excitement. This was surely God and she was 100% behind me. Ron Book heads the mission board with his wife Carolyn. They've visited BA Cameroon many times and we always get together for dinner when I'm home. They've become a great mom and dad to me in this whole mission adventure and they love my kids in Cameroon like their own. Ron texted back and said it sounded great, but how would the kids in Cameroon feel about it?

Like Alero, he spoke to my greatest fear and deepest guilt. Would they feel abandoned by me? My closest leaders in Cameroon kept sending me What's App messages, asking me what was happening and what God was saying in Kenya. I couldn't tell them. How could I say, "God is saying I'm leaving you guys to go build Bethel Atlanta Kenya?"

The next morning, I got up to pray and heard God clearly. ***"You'll always be a part of Bethel Atlanta Cameroon and will always be there to start the school, impart during the year, and then for graduation. And who said you were abandoning them? Silly girl, you're taking them with you. Unless you want to pioneer alone again..."***

My heart soared! Of course! Why would I go to a new country, all alone, and start all over again, all alone? I had a well-trained staff of powerfully gifted and prophetic teachers, intercessors, administrators, and inner healers. I had a great team for planting new schools in new nations.

I sat and wrote the name of every staff member and their greatest strengths and gifts. I also wrote their weaknesses and their greatest areas for potential growth. I prayed over each one of them and decided who I would bring with me to launch Bethel Atlanta Kenya and who was strong enough to stay behind and run Bethel Atlanta Cameroon.

I thought of Bessie – our gifted inner healer, financial and operations manager and all around stellar leader. It was hard to decide whether to take her or leave her. If I left her, I knew everything would run perfectly in Cameroon without me thinking about it. But to launch something new, I needed her, as a great leader and as a friend. She's the firm balance to my mushy mother's heart and the down-to-earth refiner to my heaven-focused visionary.

With my assistant director, Boris, there was no debate. I needed him to launch something new. Boris is pure fire and anointing. He takes the mic and bodies fall – literally. Whether he's praying, preaching, or just exhorting, people get slain in the spirit and have amazing glory encounters when Boris leads a meeting. I've never seen a young man as anointed as him. And I'm not being biased because he's my spiritual son.

Once, after he taught second year, all the staff were hanging out in the office after class. A student peeked their head in and said, "Excuse me, but what are we going to do about Mary? She's still under the table in the second year room."

We all turned to look at Boris and he gave a sheepish grin. Mary had slid under the table while Boris was teaching and lay there, shaking under the anointing for more than an hour. She had to be carried home in a taxi, moaning, "God, what are you doing to me eh? No kill me oh. Eh God, no kill me oh!" (A little pidgin for you). She was so overwhelmed by the presence of God that she was asking God not to kill her.

One day, after Boris was supposed to be ending worship, instead he started exhorting. People were getting slain everywhere. The hall was a mess of bodies strewn all over the floor under the power of

God. We had a running joke on our staff What's App page about the "management of the slain." We made a rule that the "slayer" is responsible for the slain getting home. Boris, being the primary slayer, didn't like the rule and thought the number two slayer, Bessie, should be responsible (She slays people with a hug from the Father.). I settled the argument by telling Boris to stop being a typical man, expecting a woman to clean up the mess he made. We all had a good laugh about that one.

Boris is also a gifted teacher who blows my mind with the revelation he gets. One Sunday after he preached at church service, I interrogated him about what books he'd been reading or what sermons he'd been listening to. He shrugged and said he'd just been hearing from God. I insisted that he put his revelation on the Mystery of Christ in a book. I'm sure he's full of books that we'll hopefully publish one day.

Then, of course, I have to bring my worship leader, Kingsley, who consistently brings down heaven. I want the hallmark of any Bethel Atlanta we start in any African nation to be extravagant worship and the presence. And finally, I'd bring Susan Enjema, excellent event manager, prolific teacher, intercessor, worshipper, friend and confidant.

A new level of excitement started to grow. I wasn't leaving my babies! I wasn't abandoning my school! We were going to expand and build new schools together in the nations of Africa.

The rest of the Nairobi visit was amazing. Rosie introduced me to many apostolic/prophetic, Kingdom leaders who were all excited about the prospect of Bethel Atlanta coming to Kenya. I had a sweet reunion with Apostle Peterson and enjoyed meeting his new wife and children. I got to eat Ethiopian and Indian food and drank plenty of tea and lattes. I got to go to a music and arts festival and a live music event much like the ones I went to in Atlanta. I didn't rest as much as I needed to, but I had a great time and fell even more in love with Kenya.

When I got back to Cameroon, I was still nervous about telling my kids about the outcome of my trip. Susan, who's been with me since my very first trip to Cameroon, came to see me the day after I got back. She had been the main one asking what God was saying while I was in Kenya and I knew she was prophetic enough to suspect what was coming.

I was tentative and nervous and tried to figure out how to tell her what was going on. She made it easy for me. She blurted out, "You're moving to Kenya, aren't you?"

I was shocked! I shouldn't have been. When you raise prophetic people, that's the kind of thing that happens all the time.

I told her everything that had happened on my trip and all I was dreaming about. When I told her about taking a team with me to launch, she said, "Now it makes sense!"

God had been talking to her about mentoring the junior staff and any third year students that showed promise in ministry. She had been reading books and watching videos about mentoring for a couple of weeks before I came home. God had already started dealing with her about becoming her absolute best and raising up the junior staff to be able to run the school. I was encouraged by her response and felt more encouraged about telling the rest of the staff.

That weekend, we were headed into our staff retreat to prepare to launch Year 7 of BASSM-C. I wanted to meet with the Executive Staff – my top four leaders – first to tell them about the possibility of Bethel Atlanta Kenya. I'd tell the rest of the staff in the "State of the School Address."

But I hadn't heard from Steve Hale, my Senior Leader yet. I didn't want to tell them when I didn't even have permission to move forward. I believe that a lot of the favor on my life is because I try to live by the culture of honor and respect my leadership in all that I do.

The morning the staff retreat was to kick off, I woke up to a text message from Steve Hale. Somehow, he runs a business full time and successfully pastors Bethel Atlanta church and BASSM. His life is busy, so sometimes his responses are a little delayed. I was excited and nervous to read his text.

It is a season of building and expansion. It's prophetic to see your future in Kenya and apostolic to go build it. I do believe it's your destiny to continue to build. If you have time, please share some more on how you've settled on Kenya as the next stop.

My heart leaped! He didn't believe I was crazy! He believed it was God!

I called the executive staff into the bedroom. We were all sleeping in our guesthouse for the retreat. I slowly told them about my plans for us launching Bethel Atlanta Kenya. I had already told Bessie, who in her ever nonchalant way, said, "Hmmm…sounds okay." You never get much more enthusiastic of a response from her than that. I told them that God had already spoken to Sue and about our discussion the day before.

Boris said, "No wonder! God told me the other day that my single, most important priority this year is raising up the junior staff and pouring into them so they can grow. I had no idea why."

Kingsley stared blankly at each of us and said, "I guess I'm not in the Spirit because I had no clue! I didn't see this coming!"

We all laughed and excused him for not being "in the Spirit" because he was in the middle of planning his wedding. We all discussed Bethel Atlanta

Kenya with much excitement and anticipation. This would be the crew I would take with me to launch.

I expressed my concern about telling the junior staff. They agreed that since they wouldn't be the ones to get to travel, they wouldn't be as excited about the Kenya move and might feel abandoned by us. Sue, with her beautiful mother heart, thought of a way to break the news to them. It sounded so good, I assigned her the task of telling them right after I discussed the upcoming expansion.

We went out to the parlor to meet the others for worship before the State of the School address. Worship was explosive as always. After things calmed down and the anointing lifted, I was ready to start my talk. I planned to talk about Year 7 at BASSM-C and at the very end, I planned to break the news about Bethel Atlanta Kenya.

Just before I started talking, Pastor Sako raised his hand. He said, "I have to share what I just saw while we were worshipping. Please Madame (their nickname for me – long story), I see you and Pastor Carine going to another country in Africa. I saw Boris and Kingsley traveling to another country and I saw Bessie and Sue going to yet another country. God says this is a time of expansion and don't be afraid to plant new branches of Bethel Atlanta Cameroon in other cities."

Me and the executive staff members stared at each other – completely floored.

Henry, another junior staff member raised his hand and said, "Oh, wow. I saw almost the exact same thing! You guys were sent out in two's, going to different nations in Africa."

Merlin, another junior staff member, raised his hand and said, "I dreamed the same thing the other night. I saw Boris and Kingsley, Bessie and Sue, and Please Madame and somebody else traveling and going to different nations."

I was completely done in. The newest junior staff member, Edmond, raised his hand and said, "Please Madame, remember how I gave you a prophetic word a few months back and God showed me that you would be taking some of us to go to Kenya?"

Me and the executive staff just sat there, staring at each other. The room was quiet for a few minutes.

I finally broke the silence. "Well, I was going to announce this at the end, but since God has already shown you guys, I might as well say it." I explained everything about my trip to Kenya and how God was calling us to launch Bethel Atlanta in Kenya and eventually in other nations in Africa.

The room erupted into crazy, loud praise! What in my mind was going to be a difficult, painful conversation filled with disappointment and feelings of abandonment had turned into a praise party! God is amazing. I know He was laughing at me and all my worries and fears. And I was laughing right along with Him.

Every staff member pledged to grow and press into God and be the best, most fiery revivalist they could be. We pledged together to press into God to take the nations of Africa. The last day of the staff retreat, we had one of our most explosive worship sessions ever. Everyone said their deepest "yes" to God and He birthed in us big collective dreams about taking the nations of Africa.

Eighteen

The launch of Year 7 of Bethel Atlanta Cameroon was exciting. My staff was on board with our plans for expansion. We had a good-sized first, second, and third year class. The worship was more explosive than ever from the very first week of school. My staff was functioning at their highest level ever and I realized they were ready for me not to be there full time. Some of the junior staff were teaching my subjects as good as or better than me (still not sure how I feel about that…) and everyone did their best to help me realize they'd be fine running the school most of the year without me.

Everything at BASSM-C was the best ever, but deep down on the inside, I wasn't okay. My soul was still tired and broken. All the deaths and losses had me constantly nervous and fearful of bad news. Thinking of starting a brand new school in a whole new country terrified and exhausted me. I sat down for one of my special "parlor talks" with Sue.

She and Bessie are more than staff. They're good friends and have become a safe place where I can share my heart. They know me well and are familiar with my moods and ups and downs. She asked me a bunch of coaching type questions and finally said, "Why are you in such a rush? If you're this tired and not settled in your heart, why not put Kenya off for another year?"

I reminded her of one of the prophetic words I had gotten in Kenya that had fostered the sense of urgency.

> *You don't have six months to pray about this or one month to fast about it. When you get back to Cameroon, you need to start putting things in order for this to start happening. This is the time.*

After we laughed at the prospect of me fasting for a whole month, she said, "God knows your heart and what you can handle. If it's too much, just put it on the shelf for now. He loves you and you're the most important thing to Him. Not Bethel Atlanta Kenya."

So I put it on the shelf.

That lasted for about a good week. Remember I mentioned that God gives missionaries grace to be able to tolerate the conditions they find themselves in on the mission field? For the next week, it felt like Daddy God lifted that blanket of grace. Everything drove me crazy! Completely and totally crazy!

In that week, I experienced more fatigue, frustration, and downright disgust than I ever have since I moved to Africa. And I've been in some difficult situations and some yucky places.

In those frustrated moments, I kept getting flashes of moments in Kenya – all my favorite scenes. Eating a gourmet, healthy meal at a beautiful, Edenic outdoor restaurant, the Arbor, where I wrote the first third of this book in one day because of the beauty, peace and great coffee. The fun time me and Rosie had at the Ethiopian restaurant, eating the spicy food with our hands and laughing because Rosie was being Rosie. The days daydreaming and people-watching at the tea shop. The arts and music festivals with the young, artistic creatives I got prophetic words about mentoring in the future.

I told God, "I know what you're doing. First of all, thanks for the grace you've given me these last six years. I didn't realize how much you were doing to make it possible for me to live here. Secondly, I WANT to go to Kenya. I asked You first, remember? But I can't like this. I'm tired. BA-Cameroon was a lot of work and took a lot of money to build. I don't know if I have the energy to do that again. Is this gonna be hard?

"You'll be fine. I'll take good care of you. It's going to be one of the greatest seasons of your life, filled with so much joy and fulfillment. You can't even begin to imagine how much you're going to love it."

I felt His overwhelming peace. I gave Him my heart again and my willingness to plant BA-Kenya. He gave me back my blanket of grace to live and thrive in Cameroon.

But I still needed something. There was a restlessness and tiredness in my soul that I couldn't chase away with worship, prayer, tongues, and fun times with my kids or anything that usually worked. I told God I needed something ridiculously fun and fulfilling for the Sherri side of me. Kenya was supposed to be my break from ministry where I could just be "the girl" Sherri. Instead, I was shouldered with an apostolic assignment to a new nation. Could I do something that was just fun? Please?

I felt His smile when I asked, but I had nothing in mind to do. I asked Him to show me what I needed and left it at that. What He ended up doing still blows my mind! Let me give a little backstory before I tell you.

I had just finished writing a book with my writing partner, Rhonda McKnight, called *Love A Little*. In it, the main character flies to Kenya for her sister's wedding and gets stuck on a romantic, 24-hour layover in Paris. I finished the book right before leaving for Kenya. We did a lot of research on what one would do in Paris for 24 hours and I was enthralled. As I wrote the Paris scenes, I whispered a thought – *God, I would love to go to Paris some day.*

While in Kenya talking on the phone with Alero, I got excited as we dreamed of raising up revivalists in many nations in Africa to invade the 7 Spheres of Influence. After we hung up, I whispered to God, *I would LOVE to go to London to spend some more time with Alero and give some meat to this dream.*

Not too long after I returned to Cameroon, my bestie from college messaged me. She had taken me to South Beach for a vacation the year before and wanted to go on another trip together summer of 2016. Somehow things didn't come together, so we didn't get to go anywhere. In late September, she messaged me and said, *Hey, I still want us to go on a trip together this year. Are you free right before Thanksgiving?*

Yeah, I should be able to get away. Where do you want to go?

She said she would dream up something for us and get back to me.

A few days later, she sent me a message. *I've got a great idea. Let's do Paris and London!*

At this point, if you aren't convinced you want to live in the God Zone, there's really no hope for you!

I was too shocked. I had whispered a desire to go to both London and Paris, but I wouldn't even call it praying. It was a whispered thought, lasting only for a second. Honestly, they were more wishes than anything, seeing that I had no money. I was broker than broke. I had spent more than I planned in Kenya and a lot of other unexpected expenses had taken my last personal reserves.

I'm not an irresponsible person when it comes to money. Never have been. In college, medical school, and when I worked as a doctor, I lived by a very disciplined budget and always had savings. In the last six years, God has taught me complete and total dependence on Him financially. I always have enough and things are always paid on time, but there are moments when the account is dangerously low. I know there's a miracle on the way, but at that moment, there's nothing extra to spend.

This was one of those moments. My bestie had just taken her own leap of faith and quit her job to take her own journey into destiny (Five of my close friends have done that in the past two years and it's pretty exciting to watch them.). She couldn't foot the whole bill like in South Beach. I actually preferred it that way. I'm still not good at receiving from others – it's quite painful actually. Every time she pulled out her card in South Beach and I just sat there watching her pay, I felt awful. When you've lived as a doctor, you're the one used to pulling out the card. My pride stung for most of that trip.

So why did I think I could go to Paris and London?

I asked God about it and He said to borrow the money for my part of the expenses and He would get it back to me.

Ugh, God. You're taking this trust thing too far!

I HATE borrowing, almost as bad as begging – I mean asking for donations. Especially for something as frivolous as a trip to Europe. He assured me I would have the money to pay back before Christmas. So I got excited about how He was going to do that.

I booked my plane tickets, thinking of my spiritual daughter I hadn't seen in two years because she got married and moved to Switzerland with her new husband. Winnie Khamal, the fashion designer, was now Winnie Nkwetiyim, wife and mother to the most adorable six month-old baby boy, who I had only seen pictures of. I checked on tickets to Zurich from London and they were cheap. If God was gonna bless me with mystery money, I might as well make it a European tour. Of course, I asked Him first. Remember what I said about wisdom, faith, finances and intimacy.

I was able to leave Cameroon in early November instead of December like I usually did. My staff was more than capable of running things while I fed my tired soul and fulfilled my wanderlust.

Europe was more amazing than I imagined. We stayed right in the center of Paris, across the street from the Garden of Tulles at the Louvre. We wanted to be free to eat whatever we wanted, so we took walking tours all over the city. My Fitbit registered eight to nine miles a day. We had the best croissants, omelets, and French coffee for breakfast every day and decadent meals every night and walked all over the city seeing everything a tourist wants to see in Paris. I'll restrain myself here, lest I end up giving you a full tour of Paris.

Over great meals, we caught up on life and the state of our hearts and our dreams. We laughed about our frustrations with the aging process. Kathy and I have been best friends since I was seventeen. We've always talked for hours about anything and everything. We ask each other challenging questions to make sure we're being our truest and best self. We inspire each other to take the best care of ourselves – body, soul, and spirit. We know each other so well, we're able to help each other get the right answer to any dilemma.

As I was telling her about my new dreams of launching in Kenya, she asked a lot of questions. She wanted to know whether I got a salary and was shocked when I told her I lived on donations.

I talked about all the miraculous provision I had experienced over the years, but as a best friend would, she seemed concerned. She asked about my retirement and I told her I had invested it all in BA Cameroon. The more I explained about God being Jehovah Jireh, the more worried she looked. She finally said, "Well, it's refreshing that you don't worry about your retirement. I worry about mine all the time. It must be freeing not to even have to think about it."

That struck a place in me. Remember, I'm still in this dark season where death has been too frequent and my confidence in God has been deeply affected. Moving into the new building left us in a less than comfortable place financially. I had just spent too much in Kenya and was BORROWING money for the meal I was eating. I've never been financially irresponsible, but all of a sudden, I felt like a complete lunatic.

What forty-seven year-old, responsible adult lives on donations and has no plans whatsoever for retirement? What was I really doing with my life? Living from financial miracle to donation to financial miracle with no real stability? For the first forty years of my life, I thought just like her. Work hard, save, store away for your retirement, plan, be responsible and live WISE! That's how my dad raised us.

I had a real crisis of faith in that moment in that expensive Paris café. Again, remember this is a dark season where all the enemy needed was a little crack in the door to get me spiraling downward into a deep pit of fear, doubt, and unbelief.

I started making plans in my head for how I was going to get my life together and become a financially responsible adult. Well, as many plans as you can make when you walk away from your career and have no means of supporting yourself other than your faith in God. I don't even have a medical license anymore. So the plans didn't go far. How could they? Instead, I fell into a place of fear, guilt over my lack of responsibility, and panic about what I would do for the rest of my life.

Did I need to give up these crazy pipe dreams about taking the nations of Africa, and get a real job and be a responsible adult?

nineteen

I carried this weight on the train from Paris to London. Our first night there, we met a good friend, Cherlene Wilson, who I had met while she was a on a trip from BSSM to BASSM. We later stayed together when I went out to Bethel Church for a conference and have maintained a friendship over the years. She had returned to her home in London after completing first, second, third year and an internship at BSSM in Redding.

It was interesting being in conversation with the two of them at the same time, like observing very different parts of myself interacting. Kathy is my intellectual, doctor side that loves logic, wisdom, stability and planning. Cherlene, or Cecie represents the wild and crazy, faith-filled, supernatural side of me that lives a life of ridiculous, illogical adventure.

The funniest moment of our evening was the moment when Cecie described the day when her father passed away, and she went to resurrect him from the dead. Kathy didn't even blink, even though I knew that kind of talk was foreign to her. The conversation between the two of them reflected the inner conversation going on inside of me. The logical doctor side was vying for a life of "wisdom" and stability, while the wild, supernatural side wanted to continue pressing into a life of abandoned faith.

As we left the restaurant and strolled down the street a little, Cecie pointed and said, "There's a church there, Holy Trinity Brampton. It's really Kingdom and a lot of cool stuff goes on there."

I nodded, but didn't think much more about it.

The next day, Kathy and I went on a six-hour walking tour to many famous sites in London. With the two parts of me warring inside, I didn't enjoy it as much as I had Paris. How could I enjoy being frivolous and irresponsible, enjoying Europe like I actually had a job?

Then something totally random happened. While walking to the London Eye, I saw a familiar face. I screamed, "Pat!"

He screamed, "Sherri!"

It was Pat Barrett of the worship group, Housefires. We had graduated from the first year at BASSM together. I hadn't seen him in seven years. We both laughed about how random and crazy it was to run into each other in London when we both lived in Atlanta. I congratulated him on winning the Dove award for "Good, Good, Father" and told him it was one of BA Cameroon's favorite songs.

He thanked me and said, "Hey, I'm not sure what your plans are, but we're doing a worship thing at Holy Trinity Brampton tonight. If you're free, you should come."

"A worship thing sounds great! I'll be there." I might not have gone if I didn't know the church was down the street from my hotel, as Cecie had shown us the night before.

I was exhausted though. By the time we finished our tour, my Fitbit registered nine miles. But my soul needed that worship thing. I was still feeling that broken pain of the dark season of the last two years, now with added uncertainty about my future, and guilt about my financial status.

The concert opened with a video called, "Kingdom Come," a spoken word piece with rousing images about the "broken ones" – the laid down lovers who completely give their lives to God. As the artist "spit" the words, he told my life's story of sacrifice, laying down everything to chase after God, being head over heels in love with the Father and being willing to give my life for whatever He asked me to do. The piece was amazingly written, set to inspiring pictures, and had Kingdom overtones.

My heart exploded in my chest. It was as if the piece was personally written for me and I could hear the Father and all of heaven cheering me on. I remembered the encounter when Father God warned me about defining success from heaven's perspective and not earth's.

It wasn't random at all, me meeting Pat at the London Eye. And it wasn't just about a worship thing. God went out of His way to quickly end the attack of the enemy against my heart and mind. He overwhelmingly validated my life choices and celebrated who I've become. I was right where I was supposed to be, doing exactly what I was supposed to do.

The concert was amazing – full of glory and presence. London is such an international city, and as I looked around the room at the people of all ages, nations, colors, and races, I realized God was answering that heart dream I had whispered in the Massai village. I wanted to worship with His kingdom people all over the world. I experienced that at Holy Trinity Brampton that night.

Anywhere I find myself in the Kingdom stream always feels like home to my heart. The lyrics to all the songs continued to pierce and heal my heart. By the time Housefires sang "Good, Good, Father," I got lost in a place of worship that brought another degree of healing to my heart.

After the concert though, I realized I didn't feel so good. I knew that walking miles and miles all over Europe in the cold after leaving the African heat was taking a toll on my body. I told Kathy I wanted to rest the next day while she went to high tea.

I did more than rest. I slept on and off for about thirty hours. That's unusual for me. I'm not much of a sleeper. The more I slept, the worse I felt. I stayed in the hotel room the whole day. That night, I woke up with my clothes soaked from fever. Kathy was to head home that next morning and I was going to Alero's house for a few days before heading to Zurich.

I took some Tylenol, reassured Kathy I was fine and sent her off to the airport and got in an Uber to go to West London.

Let me give a little more history on this Alero person I keep talking about. We met briefly in Nigeria while I was at that Randy Clark conference. Over lunch, she mentioned she would be in Atlanta for a few months later that year. I told her she had to go to Bethel Atlanta while she was there and gave her the church's information.

The conversation was brief, but there was something about her. She's beautiful with the most engaging smile and she seemed like someone I would get to know if she didn't live in London and me in Cameroon. She was pioneering in the Education Mountain.

Four months later, when I went home for Christmas, the Sunday I was to preach at Bethel Atlanta, I saw a beautiful, chocolate face with a radiant smile pass by as we were giving offering. She smiled and waved. I smiled and waved back, but my brain had a moment of confusion. Then it clicked – it was Alero from London who I met in Nigeria!

She had, by "random coincidence" come to Bethel Atlanta the Sunday I was preaching. She was in Atlanta because her daughter had had a car accident two years prior and ended up with a spinal cord injury. She was receiving treatment at the Shepherd Spinal Center in Atlanta after completing Project Walk in California. They had also been to Bethel Redding for prayer.

We exchanged numbers after service and planned to meet for dinner. That 7 pm dinner lingered into 2 am tea. We talked the whole night like we'd been friends forever. I felt a divine connection and as we talked about everything from our plans to raise revivalists all over Africa to our love lives and love lost, and our personal dreams, our hearts became knitted in a way that only God can do.

I'll stop for a minute to say that when you become a missionary, you become somewhat homeless – meaning no country feels like home. After living in Africa for many years, America feels materialistic and plastic to me. It's familiar and comfortable, but even with my family and friends there, it no longer completely fits and I no longer feel at home there.

I love my new family in Cameroon and our beautiful community of love, worship, and God chasing, but the poverty, deaths, hopelessness and corruption make it not feel like home either.

In Alero, I found home. She's West African, so understands the culture that has affected my very

DNA. I could break out in pidgin English, and not have to translate and explain that some things are just better said in pidgin. She's also highly educated, intellectual, artistic, and forward thinking, exposed, sophisticated and progressive. I love the way God does divine connections.

When I was burnt out and tired, the two places I wanted to go were to Nairobi, or to see Alero in London. I had actually priced tickets the year before to see if it was feasible for me to go. I know it sounds crazy to want to fly to another country to see somebody you've had dinner with once, but ask God for your own divine connection so you can see the miracle of what it feels like when He brings people together.

That morning, at her beautiful home in London, she made me one of my favorite teas, cooked me an omelet and we talked for hours. Like five hours straight. After a while though, I felt tired and drained again, even after all that sleeping the day before. I told Alero I wanted to take a nap. She needed to go visit her father and then prepare for a dinner party she was having that evening with some other Kingdom friends.

A few minutes later, when I settled into bed, I started shivering uncontrollably. That had only happened once before – the year before when I had malaria. After about fifteen minutes of rebuking the fever, I knocked on Alero's door, shaking violently, and through chattering teeth told her I needed to go to an urgent care for probable malaria. She laid hands and prayed for me and the shivering stopped immediately, but I still felt awful.

At the urgent care, my fever was 104 and my heart rate was 136. I was pretty sick. The urgent care doctor insisted I go to the Emergency Room. She waived the $150 fee just for walking in the door and sent me to the public hospital. My doctor brain kicked in and I got real concerned when she said I was probably septic.

Alero canceled her dinner party and sat with me in the ER all night. Two of her friends who were supposed to come to the party came to the hospital to see me. When Alero had talked about her friend, Abby, who I was supposed to meet at the dinner party, I knew I had a prophetic word for her. I was mad at the devil that I was on a hard ER gurney instead of at dinner and I felt bad for ruining the party. Even though my head was spinning and I felt awful, I gave her that prophetic word.

At midnight, they told me I was too sick to go home and they would have to admit me. Admit me? To a hospital in London? My Momma was in Atlanta! I couldn't be admitted to a hospital in London. And I had already borrowed money for this trip. They said the ER visit was free, but if I got admitted, I'd have to pay.

I protested like an idiot for a while until finally the ER doc said, "You're a doctor. If you were me, would you let you go home?"

I pouted for a few seconds, but admitted I wouldn't. I finally persuaded Alero to go home at one in the morning. She had left her daughter, Efena, in the house all by herself for the whole evening without their much needed nightly caregiving rituals.

They rolled me to my room at 3:30 in the morning, full of antibiotics and fluids, but also fears about what was wrong with me.

Twenty

After thirty minutes in that hospital room in London, I thought to myself, *This is going in a book.* There were four beds in the room, separated by thin, blue curtains. None of my roommates for the night were asleep. An elderly woman in the bed next to me was alternating between making baby noises and animal noises and giving the nurses a fit, trying to get out of the bed. The patient in the bed next to me alternated between yelling for pain medicine and snoring, arguing with the nurse that she was in too much pain to sleep. The final patient was pacing back and forth, holding two different bags draining two different colors of fluid. I'll spare you the whole description, but she must have had some sort of bowel surgery.

I couldn't believe this crazy, 3-ring circus was where I was supposed to rest and recuperate for the next day or so. I panicked, wondering how long they would make me stay.

I lay awake, unable to sleep because of all the noise, and having difficulty breathing because of a cough that had gotten progressively worse over the past two days. Later in the morning, a doctor came in with a large team of residents and medical students. I was the case of the day.

Forty-seven year-old medical doctor who's spent the last six years in Africa presents with fever, tachycardia, and elevated CRP. Working diagnosis – infection of unknown origin.

They had run every test in the book for every exotic disease they could think of. I felt better after fluids and IV antibiotics and wanted to be released out of the crazy hospital back to Alero's sweet, presence-filled house.

By the afternoon, the infectious disease specialist came in with a computer on a stand to discuss my results with me. As he scrolled through pages and pages of lab tests, a cash register was "cha chinging" in my head. With my knowledge of medicine in America, I knew what this hospital stay could possibly cost and my heart seized with panic. He finally admitted what I told them when I came into the ER. I'd said I had either malaria or pneumonia. He showed me my abnormal X-ray and told me that since my fever was gone and I was stable, they could discharge me the next day on oral antibiotics. I begged to be released that day and promised to be a good patient and come back for follow-up. He said he'd think about it.

I knew all the doctors were disappointed that this Africa-exposed traveler only had a simple pneumonia. They were probably hoping for some exciting, exotic tropical disease. I know I would have been disappointed. But me, the patient, was happy to have a clear diagnosis, treatment plan, and to be going home the next day.

But then I thought of all the labs the doctor had scrolled through. He was an infectious disease specialist and I knew he had to have a high consulting fee. The regular medical doctor would need his cut, too. The dollar signs – or pound signs in this case – were adding up in my head. The infectious disease doctor told me the administrator would be there soon with the bill and they would need a payment plan before discharging me.

I panicked. I was on a vacation with money I had borrowed! I didn't have money for the thousands of dollars this hospitalization was going to cost!

My mom sent me an audio Vox to make sure I was fine. In my emotional, sleep-deprived, breathless state, I told her I was fine, but not sure how I would pay this bill. My parents already provide great support for me and the work in Cameroon, so I didn't want to ask them for anything more, even though they'd gladly give their right arm for me.

My mom, knowing me all too well, tried to calm me down. "People love you dear, and are always looking for ways to support you. You'll just raise the money when you get home."

I didn't mean to yell at Mommy, but I did. "But any money I raise needs to go to BA Cameroon and BA Kenya! Not a stupid hospital bill!" She tried to speak sweet Mommy words to calm me down, but I blurted out something else and hung up our conversation.

I didn't want to yell at Mommy anymore. I went after the real source of my frustrations and yelled at God.

"I can't believe You ruined my vacation. I can't believe I'm in the hospital. You know I can't pay for this! Why did this happen? You're supposed to be taking care of me and watching over me. You know our financial state. Now I gotta raise thousands of dollars for a hospital bill?!"

Poor God. I went on and on for a while, yelling at Him in my mind until the administrator walked in.

I was so emotional I almost asked her to come back until I got myself together. She started talking about the bill and their billing procedures and how she hoped I could pay the balance that day. I panicked again. Did she think I could just swipe my credit card for thousands of dollars?

She put a sheet of paper in front of me. "In our medical system, you get everything for a flat fee. All the labs, medications, doctor fees – everything is included. The daily rate is 790 pounds, but since you came in early this morning, if you're discharged before tomorrow, it'll be 545 pounds."

Were my ears hearing her correctly? I stared down at the paper and did the math in my head. If they sent me home, the bill, which I thought would be in the thousands, was going to be about $650?

I Voxed mom and had her transfer some money into my account and paid the bill. The woman left and I had to face God.

"God, I'm soooooo sorry. Please forgive me. I'm so terrible."

I apologized in tears for about twenty minutes. He patted me on my back and told me it was okay, but I felt awful. I needed this dark season to be over so my heart could be healed. I know God loves and forgives me, but I hate treating Him so bad.

I tried to get myself settled in for the evening to sleep. It had been thirty hours since I'd slept and I was exhausted from all the emotions and the illness. When the nurses came, I asked if they could give me something to sleep that evening. My roommates had been crunk all day and I was sure they would keep me up all night again. If I didn't get some sleep, it would take longer for me to get better.

I know I whined when I asked, "So the doctor didn't say I could go home?"

The nurse replied. "Oh no, you were discharged about an hour ago. I figured you'd want to stay until tomorrow and rest."

Seriously lady???

I was too happy to be discharged to be angry. I jumped out of bed, got dressed, and told Alero I'd be there soon. I waited for them to bring me all the discharge medicines included in that flat fee. This missionary was grateful for socialized medicine.

As I rode in the taxi to Alero's, tears slid down my face. I was happy and relieved to be going "home," but I still felt awful for the way I had treated God.

I whispered a prayer. "God, I know You've forgiven me, but I'm still so sorry. Please, You have to heal us. I can't be in this space anymore. I need this dark season to be over. I don't want to be afraid and doubtful and angry at You. Please heal my heart. Please, heal us...please..."

When I got to Alero's house, all I wanted to do was sleep. But she insisted I join her and Efena for dinner. We sat and talked for a while and then Efena wheeled into the kitchen in her snazzy wheelchair to join us.

We talked and laughed and ate. I was still breathing fast and coughing a lot and was exhausted, but enjoyed their company. We sat up for four hours talking. It was beautiful to watch the bond between mother and daughter. During their time of rehab at Project Walk in California, Alero had turned it into an adventure for Efena.

Efena is a gifted writer and aspires to write for television and movies. Alero took her on a fabulous Hollywood tour. I had seen most of it on Facebook, but hearing them relive it with so much excitement and joy made me feel like I was on the trip with them.

Alero and Efena talked of miracle after miracle God had done in the time since her accident. Miracles of provision, healing, fun, and special times together on their adventures in California. I watched them banter, finishing each other's sentences, full of sheer joy, speaking of God's goodness to them.

Alero has traveled all over the world, has her Master's from Sloan School of Business in London, has served in the Minister of Education's cabinet in Nigeria, has started a bank, has launched an Education Hub to raise up revivalists in the Education mountain in Nigeria and has dreams of raising up revivalists all over Africa. She's brilliant, articulate, and possesses the gifts necessary to transform lives and nations, but in that moment, she was a mother. She's sacrificed everything to devote her entire life to her daughter.

Efena, who has fought for her life and has fought to walk for two years, is one of the most joyous people I've ever met – full of smiles, life, dreams, and laughter.

Watching the love and joy between them was mesmerizing. I have the best mother on the planet, but their relationship touched me deeply that night.

Finally, exhaustion took over and after midnight, we all went to bed. I lay down in the bed, grateful to finally sleep. I awoke about an hour later, feeling like someone was shaking me. After focusing for a few seconds, I realized I was the one shaking. I could barely breathe. I sat up in bed in a panic. Fearful middle-of-the-night thoughts filled my brain.

I was shaking again, which meant I must still have a fever. It wasn't pneumonia. Some exotic sickness was taking over my body and I was going to have to wake up Alero to go back to the hospital and get admitted again and they were going to have to run a whole new battery of tests and I wasn't going to make it home to my family for Thanksgiving. But they had already ordered every test and didn't find anything, which meant that whatever I had was undiagnosable. Maybe I had one of those "mysterious illnesses" that Africans get where they get a fever in the morning and die by the evening.

I was going to die. Right there in the bed in Alero's house in London. I was surely dying and was about to break my parents' hearts. I should have never gone to Africa, the land of malaria and demons...

Doctor brain, writer's imagination and sleep deprivation are a very dangerous combination in the wee hours of the morning.

I felt Father God sit down on the bed next to me. He started rubbing my back. ***"Calm down, babygirl. You're okay. You're fine. Calm down. Breathe. You're okay."***

He sat rubbing my back and talking comforting words to me for a few minutes. My breathing slowed down and with Him there, the panic left.

"You can't sleep lying flat with pneumonia, my love. You're not dying. You just weren't getting enough oxygen to your brain. You're fine. Just breathe. Calm down."

After I was calm, I apologized for being so afraid. Again...

I sat there for a while, catching my breath and apologizing for my doubts and fears. Then I asked the question that had been on my mind. Why had I come to Alero's in London? If I had gone home when Kathy did, I would have been at home with my Mommy when I got sick.

"I thought I came here to talk about the 7 Mountains and to strategize how to take over Africa. Instead I got sick. Why am I here? Did I mess up? Should I have gone home? Did I miss You?"

He sat there for a second and finally said, *"Did you enjoy your time with Alero and Efena?"*

I smiled. "Yeah, they're great. Thanks for that."

He asked, *"Don't you love the way they love each other?"*

I was overwhelmed and suddenly could feel His immense love for them. Tears started trickling down my cheeks. "I did. It's incredible." Tears continued to stream. I could feel His love flowing into the room and it was getting thick and heavy, tangible and weighty. Somehow I knew I was about to experience the encounter of my life.

He kept talking to me about Alero and Efena. I won't share it here because it was a personal word for them about how heaven sees them. After He talked about them for a while, He replayed a scene from dinner in my mind.

After we ate, Efena had left her vegetables lined up on the edge of her plate. Alero took the plate, picked up the fork and put on the perfect Mommy face. Her British, Nigerian accent was dripping with love when she said, "You're going to eat these vegetables, my dear."

She proceeded to feed Efena like a Mama bird, looking at her with eyes full of so much Mama-love. As I saw the scene again on the God screen, it was even more beautiful.

God put His hand on my back. ***"She loves her daughter so much. What if I brought you here only to see that? Would that be enough?"***

I nodded with tears flowing down my face in full force. I choked down a lump in my throat.

He then said, ***"With the love you saw, can you imagine how much I absolutely love you?"***

And then all of heaven released a huge wave of His love. It felt like an ocean, a tidal wave, a Niagara Falls of loved poured into the room and into my heart all in one eternal moment. I was sobbing – something one shouldn't do when a big part of their left lung is filled with pneumonia.

I could hardly breathe, not from the pneumonia, but because His love was so overpowering. Overwhelming, intoxicating, extravagant, pure, holy – this writer doesn't have enough words...

His love poured over me in tsunami waves, over and over and over for what felt like a sweet forever. I cried tears for every loss over the past two years. I cried out that moment when I found out I wasn't going to be a mother to a little girl I had grown to love as my own. I cried out my fears of losing those closest to me to mysterious illnesses or accidents. I cried out my fears of what would face me in Kenya. I cried out the fatigue and frustration.

Father God completely baptized me in waves of His love in that guest bedroom in West London. He healed so much of my heart that the next morning, when I woke up after only a few hours of sitting up in bed asleep, everything felt brand new.

I cried into my tea and oatmeal that I quietly prepared while Alero and Efena slept. I cried trying to tell Alero I'd had a God encounter. I cried for pretty much the whole next month.

Alero and I spent the whole day talking – not about the 7 Mountains, but sharing our hearts, our lives, and our supernatural stories of faith. She has the BEST stories of her adventures and travels all over the world. I shared stories about Bethel Atlanta Cameroon. Our hearts bonded even further.

That night, I went to sleep sitting up. I still woke up having difficulty breathing. This time I got mad at the right person. I told satan he better leave me alone because every minute of sleep I lost, I was going to spend in intercession. I started praying for some of my kids and planned to send them prophetic words the next morning. I still couldn't sleep and this time I felt Jesus come into the room. I knew I was in for another encounter.

I won't share all of it, as I intend to write a book on how God encounters can change your life, but I will share the part where Jesus stood before me as a mighty King. I was overwhelmed by His sovereignty, power, glory, splendor, majesty, and Kingliness!

In the vision, I bowed on my face before Him, weeping and worshipping. Again, I could hardly breathe, I was so undone by His glory. I kept worshipping Him as King and Ruler over all the Earth. I had never experienced His magnificence to that degree.

Angels lifted me up from bowing before Him and dressed me in a royal robe and put a crown on my head. As soon as they finished adorning me, I fell down before Him, worshipping again and my golden crown fell on the ground at His feet. His majesty was more than magnificent. I thought I might explode.

I began weeping and worshipping, telling Him how worthy He is. I whispered, "Jesus, You're such a worthy King. You're worthy of my whole life, worthy of my everything. I lay down my life at Your feet. I give You my whole life and everything, all over again.

"Let this be the last time we ever have this discussion. I give You my life and I never want to take it back again. Settle it in my heart forever and ever, for all of eternity. I'm Yours. I don't care about a salary. I don't care about retirement. I belong to You. My life is Yours."

I continued to weep and surrender until I fell into a deep sleep until morning.

I wasn't quite well enough to travel yet, so I postponed my trip to Zurich for one more day and had another all-day talking session with Alero. We finally got to talk about the 7 Mountains and our hearts swelled as we shared our thoughts, ideas and dreams for how to establish the Kingdom of God in the nations of Africa. I jotted notes and we created a framework of a strategy for revolution.

Between the night encounters and the days of sharing our stories of faith and dreams about taking nations, I left London healed, restored and ready to conquer new territories. I flew to Zurich and had the best time surprising Winnie. Her husband and I had cooked up a scheme and she thought one of his friends was visiting from Paris.

She was beyond shocked to see me at her front door. I have the best video of her gasping when she saw me at the front door, then running back and forth between me and the living room, trying to figure out whether she should put the baby down or hug me. We had a great time sharing and catching up and I got rest and healed a little more from the pneumonia before taking the long flight back to Atlanta.

I was a bit nervous and a lot excited about going home to Atlanta, more so than usual. Of course I wanted to be with my family, and quell my parents' fears about me being hospitalized in a foreign country. I couldn't wait to see my friends and hang out, talk and laugh, as a peer and not as Aunty Sherri.

But most of all, I was looking forward to spending time with the Bethel Atlanta leadership. There were so many thoughts swirling in my heart and mind about Bethel Atlanta Africa. I, ever the external processor, needed to talk things out and hopefully make plans and goals out of everything I was dreaming.

Twenty-one

When I reached Atlanta, I was still exhausted from the pneumonia and all the hours of travel. I got there the day before Thanksgiving and got to enjoy sweet time with my family. I rested over the next week or so, but was itching to meet with my leadership.

At our first lunch meeting, I talked non-stop, outlining my dreams for Bethel Atlanta Africa. I was nervous, trying to read their faces to know whether they thought I was crazy, dreaming too extravagantly, and wanting to move forward too fast.

I told them about the miraculously financed trip to Kenya and all the prophetic words and apostolic conversations that happened there. I told them of the response of my staff when I returned to Cameroon and how everyone is ready to launch other schools in other nations. I told them about my conversations with Alero and the desire for Bethel Atlanta to come to Nigeria. I told them of all the different countries I wanted to reach in planning for a strategic takeover of the continent of Africa.

I cringed a little when I told them I was ready to launch KLA Kenya that summer. Would they think it was too soon? Did we need to wait and plan more?

If God told me through a prophetic word that it was urgent, would He put that on their hearts as well?

When I finally stopped to take a breath and a sip of water, I thought about everything I had just said. Was it grandiose and ridiculously impossible? Or was it radical faith to co-labor with a God whose heart is revival in the nations?

I looked around the table and my anxious eyes were met with nods and smiles. I can't remember who spoke first, but I remember the words, "Wow, that all sounds amazing."

I let out the breath I didn't realize I was holding as everyone around the table – Steve and Lindy Hale, the Senior Leaders, Lauren Brownlee, their daughter and administrator extraordinaire of all things Bethel Atlanta, and Ron and Carolyn Book, the heads of the mission department – voiced their excitement and assent.

They fully supported me and believed in us launching not only KLA Kenya, but Bethel Atlanta Kenya and even Bethel Atlanta Africa!

Each person shared their thoughts and even some experiences that made them believe the things on my heart were from God. You know you're doing life with the right people when you're going on and on about taking a whole continent and your leaders say, "Yes! Let's go for it! We want to get behind you and support you in any way we can!"

The response that soared my heart the most was, "How can we help? What do you need?"

Even though I meet with my leaders every time I'm home, I'm always unprepared when they ask that question. I sat there and thought for a moment and realized what I needed the most was some help making actual plans. It's one thing to dream, but another to actually do spreadsheets and timelines to make a dream come true. For some reason, birthing this new dream had me a little fearful, and I didn't want to plan it by myself.

About a week later, I had a meeting with some of Bethel Atlanta's strategic leaders and we sat for a few hours, birthing KLA Kenya, for real, not just in my heart. We came up with a strategic plan, including a budget, timeline, a to-do list, and a calendar for Bethel Atlanta Kenya for the next two years. I felt loved, supported and celebrated.

I got tons of prophetic words from BA friends while I was home. On the Sunday I preached, I told my church about BA Kenya and many people came up afterwards to share their excitement about our expansion and to offer support.

I put an intensive plan together to raise the $10,000 budget we came up with for KLA Kenya. I created a fundraising letter and social media posts and started posting on my social media sites. I woke up one morning, feeling a little anxious about how much money I needed to raise. I planned to get up and send letters to all of my supporters, telling them about the project and asking them to give. I planned to schedule social media posts for the next month. I wanted to take advantage of end-of-the-year giving, so knew I needed to be vigilant with posting for the next few days. I asked God for His input on how to raise the money.

His answer was clear as day. *"Just come sit in My presence and let Me do the rest."*

That unsettled me a little. I wanted to work, make things happen, do what I needed to do to bring in the money. He wanted me to just sit in His presence? What was that going to do?

But I listened. At first I was restless, because I felt like I should be doing something. But then I settled in and just enjoyed Him. We snuggled and talked and I rested in His arms for an hour or two.

When I finished, I checked my messages. I had a Facebook message from a friend and supporter at Bethel Atlanta, saying he and his wife wanted to give $5,000 for KLA Kenya. I was floored! That was half the budget! I ran around the house screaming and thanking God. We were halfway to our goal on the first day of me fundraising! I couldn't believe it!

I felt God smile. *"I told you to rest and let Me take care of it."*

The next day, I did the same thing. I rested in His arms for a couple of hours. My dad interrupted me to say there was a donation in the PayPal account for $2,000. He struggled to pronounce the person's name. I recognized the name as Nigerian, but didn't know who it was.

I checked Facebook Messenger again and there was a message from the person who sent the donation. He explained that he was a friend of Alero's and she had told him about me and Bethel Atlanta Cameroon. He had seen my posts about KLA Kenya and wanted to sow, in hopes that KLA Nigeria would be next.

I screamed and cried and danced all around the house! This was crazy! All I was doing was sitting and soaking and God was bringing in the money from places I would have never dreamed of.

I wrote my staff in Cameroon and Boris wrote back, "Hmmm…I was just praying about KLA Nigeria this morning."

When I finished chatting with them, I checked my email and a precious friend and faithful supporter had sent me a Messenger inbox. She wanted to support KLA Kenya and knew my budget was $10,000. She wanted to donate the whole amount.

I screamed so loud I scared my poor, seventy-six year-old father. I was crying so hard I couldn't explain what was wrong so just gave him my phone to read her message.

My parents have loved watching my journey of faith and are amazed at every miracle they see God do for me and Bethel Atlanta Cameroon. My dad gets a tear in his eye when he talks about how proud of me he is and how honored he is that God allowed him to raise me. Did I mention that after Daddy recovered from his near death experiences, he graduated from the first and second years of BASSM and is now a radical revivalist himself?

I stopped crying and took off running around the house, screaming and praising. I'm not one of those polished church shouters with the fancy, rhythmic steps. I'm much more goofy and crazy, running in circles and jumping up and down like an idiot. I'm pretty sure I crack the angels up with my antics. That day though, I think they were jumping and goofy dancing with me.

Other donations came in from other supporters, some well known, some I barely know and a perfect stranger that I still have no idea how we're connected. By the end of three days of simply soaking, we had raised $20,000 for KLA Kenya. I'm still overwhelmed as I'm typing this, a month later, at how loud the "Yes and Amen" of God is for this new project.

I had another exciting, but completely unexpected meeting during the holiday. When I told the leadership team about the strategic countries needed to bring revival to Africa, Ron Book mentioned a young revivalist he knew from South Africa. He said he wanted to connect the two of us.

I wasn't sure how to feel about that. We were moving forward with immediate plans for Kenya, and I could feel Alero and her friends pulling me to Nigeria. I was pretty sure I wasn't ready to add South Africa to the mix. I thought about Alero telling me God had given her three African countries. Nigeria, Kenya and South Africa. I wasn't the biggest fan of

South Africa the two times I visited. It felt so Westernized that I felt like if I was going to do ministry there, I might as well be at home in Atlanta. But she spoke of a visit to Cape Town where she had a God encounter and she knew it was a strategic place for her.

I set up the meeting with Tony Barwick, a radical, young South African revivalist, because I trust Ron, who was convinced I needed to make the connection. I didn't really expect anything to come out of it. From the moment Tony walked into Starbucks and we greeted each other and shared a hug, I felt the divine connection. We talked for two hours, straight into my next meeting, sharing our histories and what brought us to where we are, and our dreams for taking the continent of Africa.

He invited me to come train his leaders in Cape Town, in their new mission house on top of a mountain, overlooking the ocean (my kinda place!) and I invited him to come visit Bethel Atlanta Cameroon. We committed to press into God to know the purpose of our connection and to see how it could be instrumental in bringing revival to Africa.

I was stunned after the meeting and started to feel like God's plans are much more extensive and much more immediate than mine.

I also got to talk to Alero for some hours. We dreamed again of strategies for raising revivalists in Nigeria. We decided to make things more concrete than exciting conversations for hours in her kitchen or on the phone. We dreamed up a Kingdom Roundtable of leaders interested in bringing revival to Africa and set a date to convene in March of 2017 in Lagos. God blessed us with finances for me to be able to take Bessie and Boris to go with me. I'm pretty sure by the end of that meeting, we'll be strategizing KLA Nigeria.

I've had several days when I wake up overwhelmed at the prospect of it all. This year, I'll be in Nigeria, Kenya, and maybe South Africa. We'll launch KLA Kenya this year and prayerfully, KLA Nigeria soon. It's scary, overwhelming, exciting, anxiety provoking and exhilarating to think about and plan it.

Hopefully, it won't be long before I'm writing *The God Zone 2* about our adventures in Kenya and East Africa, Nigeria and Ghana in the West, and South Africa and Botswana in the South. My heart is filled with visions and dreams for establishing the Kingdom of God in the nations of Africa.

With Daddy God and all of heaven backing me, my kids from Cameroon helping me to build, Bethel Atlanta and my friends supporting and encouraging me, the best family in the world cheering for me, and YOUR prayers, I believe we'll do just that.

The End

Bio

After working for 15 years as a medical doctor, Sherri Lewis answered the call of God on her life and launched into an adventure as a full-time missionary in Africa. In 2010, she founded the Bethel Atlanta School of Supernatural Ministry-Cameroon and now in 2017, is in the process of launching Bethel Atlanta Kenya with dreams of reaching many other African countries. She loves to teach and impart on the prophetic, the message of the Kingdom, purpose and destiny and intimacy with God. She enjoys leading worship and training others in prophetic worship and dreams of raising up an army of creative Kingdom artists. She resides between Buea, Cameroon, Nairobi, Kenya, and Atlanta, GA.

82260231R00145

Made in the USA
Columbia, SC
15 December 2017